CHARLES DOWDING'S
VEG
journal

EXPERT NO-DIG ADVICE, MONTH BY MONTH

CHARLES DOWDING'S
VEG
journal

EXPERT NO-DIG ADVICE, MONTH BY MONTH

F

FRANCES LINCOLN LIMITED
PUBLISHERS

Frances Lincoln Limited
74–77 White Lion Street, London N1 9PF
www.franceslincoln.com

Charles Dowding's Veg Journal
Copyright © Frances Lincoln Limited 2014
Text copyright © Charles Dowding 2014
Photographs copyright © Charles Dowding 2014
First Frances Lincoln edition 2014

A catalogue record for this book is available from
the British Library.

ISBN 978-0-7112-3526-7

Printed and bound in China

9 8 7 6 5 4 3 2 1

Contents

Introduction

Gardening feels more fulfilling when the jobs that need doing are spread throughout the year and at their most effective time. 'Little and often' has three marvellous results:

- It becomes easier to keep on top of growth at peak times, when you can otherwise feel overwhelmed by many jobs arising as plants need tending, harvests are happening, weeds are growing and seeds want sowing.

- You spend less time overall, because jobs are completed more quickly when tackled at the right moment. This particularly applies to weeding, when you save much time through dealing with small weeds instead of large ones.

- The plot and garden look tidier and more beautiful, with an abundance of healthy growth.

To help you achieve this happy state, I will take you through a year of vegetable growing, covering the most important seasonal tasks, after explaining some important jobs that keep cropping up.

Teaching courses in my own and other gardens around the country has brought me into contact with many wonderful people, some of whom are new to gardening and some with a lifetime's experience. They all share a desire to discover easier and more productive ways of managing their plots and gardens, to enjoy more food with richer flavours and over a longer season, and to gain a better idea of 'what happens next', enabling harvests to continue through all seasons.

Many course participants offer tips of their own, which reminds me how much there is still to learn, even after three decades of experimenting with vegetables and growing large quantities for sale. Yet there is also a surprisingly simple way of growing your own food, once you get the hang of not digging and of sowing seeds in exactly their right season. Start well, allow yourself to wonder and enjoy the journey: this is the essence of what I have to teach.

No-dig success

My own situation is unusual in spanning the gap between domestic and market gardening. Although I produce a lot of vegetables, I do not feel at home with machinery and have managed to scale upwards from a few raised beds, doing everything by hand as though still in a small garden.

Key to success has been a no-dig approach, saving the time of digging and also of much weeding, because many fewer weeds grow on undisturbed soil. Fellow growers and all gardeners who continually battle to keep on top of weeds are intrigued by my soil's cleanliness. Having fewer weeds means I can manage a larger garden and look after the soil more carefully.

Searching for a combination of economic viability and high quality of food has led me to try many ways of enhancing soil fertility. I find that growth and quality are improved by simply covering my beds with 2.5–5cm (1–2in) of compost over their surface, which means two-thirds of the total area each year (paths and beds' sloping sides make up the other third).

Vegetables are hungry plants. Whatever their eventual size, we spend the same amount of time sowing, planting and weeding them, so it makes sense to maintain soil at a highly productive level.

This book is distilled from my experience of thirty bountiful years during which I have tried out many ways of maintaining soil, sowing seed, controlling weeds, watering plants and harvesting produce. It is a concentrated summary of all my successes and failures. Mistakes have been a particularly useful, if painful, help in establishing the possibilities for achieving more abundant harvests.

Keeping track of my many summer sowings.

JANUARY

JANUARY can be even more
wintry than December, but
there are often a few fine
days to do jobs, even if they
are not urgent. Winter is a
time for getting ahead, and
for generating plans and
ideas for the season *in situ*,
among your beds and plants
as you do some gardening.

'My advice is simple: disturb your soil as little as possible.'

Soil preparation simplified

The usual recommendation is to dig or even double dig the soil for growing vegetables. Because this is repeated so many times, most gardeners accept the task without wondering if it is really necessary. In fact there is no need to dig at all, and my comparisons of growth on dug and undug soil in adjacent beds have revealed to me the temporary harm done by soil cultivation. Undug beds grow more abundantly in spring, while the dug soil is recovering from being dug, before it catches up in autumn. The dug beds have more weeds and are less easy to water because their clay surface tends to smear and cap. So

my advice is simple: disturb your soil as little as possible, though sometimes you may have to, as when digging parsnips, planting trees and removing some large weeds. Initial clearance of weedy and grassy ground can mostly be achieved with mulches such as cardboard and compost, and some digging out of woody plants. Thereafter, keep the surface clean by looking for weeds, and pulling or hoeing them at all times – a regular task that becomes easy once soil settles down to an undisturbed life.

Friends in the soil

Soil is alive with helpful bacteria, fungi, worms, beetles etc., which appreciate being fed with composted organic matter on a regular basis. I spread 2.5–5cm (1–2in) on the surface of my beds every year, mostly as I clear plants in the late autumn. Surface compost weathers to a soft mulch over winter and can be directly sown or planted into.

Making and sourcing enough compost to spread on all beds every year is a worthwhile aim, because it increases harvests and also the ease of gardening. Think of it as feeding the soil, rather than feeding plants. The insoluble nutrients in organic matter on top of undug soil become accessible to plants through a proliferation of mycorrhizal fungi, and the compost mulch conserves moisture.

Year-old compost is soft, crumbly and alive.

Spreading compost between rows of carrots in May.

Soil does not need to be mixed, stirred, scraped or tickled. Only large lumps of organic matter on top require some knocking around with a fork or rake in order to create an even surface, mostly in winter and spring.

Clean soil

Weeds are a cause of aggravation to many gardeners, yet they can be made simple to deal with. Once soil is clean of most weed seeds, sowing and growing become easier and more enjoyable. There are three stages to this:

1. Clear the ground of existing woody plants. Either you can then mulch weeds, for different lengths of time according to which weeds are present; or clear them by hand, or even hoe them off if the soil is dry.
2. Pull or hoe all new weeds when small, long before they flower and create new seeds. Regrowth of perennial weeds such as creeping grasses and bindweed needs regular removal with a trowel, with the aim of weakening roots so that, with one or two exceptions, they disappear completely.
3. Soil that is left undug and has some well-rotted organic matter spread on top is in a calm and fertile state which, in my experience, reduces the need for weeds to grow. The few that do are easier to remove.

Less feeding and watering

When growing in undisturbed, well-nourished soil, plants can access nutrients as needed. No extra feeding of vegetables is necessary. Only container-grown plants require regular feeding, as well as watering.

In open soil, watering plants in undug soil with a compost mulch on the surface is no more than an occasional job. New plants need watering in once or twice, and are then best left alone to send roots downward. Subsequent watering is most effective when done thoroughly and with long intervals between.

Simple rotation

A mantra of much gardening advice is the principle of four-yearly rotation. Although a sound idea, this is often impractical, especially in small plots. Instead, I advise simply that you grow exactly what you want to eat, with some planning before the season begins. Make a list – then look up when each vegetable needs to be sown, how much space it will take up and how long it needs to grow. You will notice that many harvests occur in late spring and early summer, such as salads, spinach, carrots, early potatoes and garlic. After you have harvested these you can then sow or plant the free ground again for an autumn or winter harvest.

In terms of rotating plants to minimize their exposure to pest and disease, I recommend simply keeping as long a time interval as you can between vegetables of the same families (see page 168), because of their potential vulnerability to the same problems.

This results in 'rotations' of different lengths. For instance, in my gardens, where I grow a lot of salad, there are sometimes only two years between crops of the lettuce family, compared with about four years between vegetables of the onion family (alliums) and ten years between potatoes. The gaps change in length as I grow more or less of certain vegetables every year.

Companion planting

There are benefits of close relationships among particular plants. Long ago I witnessed the extra growth of Brussels sprout plants with some lettuce planted between them, compared to the slower growth of those with empty soil between. However, companion planting is sometimes misrepresented as a panacea for most ills. My vegetables have suffered damage when supposedly protected by companions, as with onions against carrot fly, marigolds against aphids and carrots against leek moth. I still grow beautiful marigolds with tomatoes, just without any expectation that all pests will disappear.

Health in the garden

Healthy plants have a beautiful bloom and their harvests are more nutritious and long lived than those of unhealthy plants. Successful gardening happens when one concentrates on health rather than disease. An analysis of healthy soil might find all sorts of bacteria we are uncomfortable with, but they belong in the soil, and the point is that they help plants to grow healthily. Soil is full of hard-working, useful bacteria, fungi and nematodes: wonderful growth happens when we understand and encourage the organisms that encourage soil and plant health. Disease-causing organisms may also be present in healthy soil, but they can only take hold when health is absent, or when plants are dying off at the end of their growing cycle, at which point disease is a necessary part of the recycling process.

Spreading home-made compost in October, on a bed just cleared of beans.

Tools you need

Gardening involves the repeated use of a few simple tools, so buy the best you can afford, or look out for well-crafted, old ones. Much of what is deemed necessary for gardening is really in the category of gadgets or luxuries, but this list highlights the tools and accessories you really need. My favourite tools are made of copper (in fact, 95 per cent copper and 5 per cent tin); the metal is strong, not magnetic, and does not rust. This is a keen advantage for trowels, hoes and spades, where smooth, sharp blades make for effortless use, and there is no need for any regular cleaning or oiling.

You will need

1-2 BUCKETS: For collecting weeds, crop residues and slugs and for carrying water and bringing home harvests.

A manure fork (on right) has longer handle and prongs than a garden one.

A DIBBER: For making holes of about the same size as root balls of plants grown in plugs and modules, onion sets, garlic cloves and even potato tubers at planting out time. You can dib holes quickly and then fill them with whatever you are planting. The dibbers I recommend are spade handles with a pointed end, usually in wood. Most dibbers are too short to offer much leverage and also it is difficult to create a pattern of planting holes with so little perspective. Make your own quite easily, from a wooden handle about 75cm (30in) long: chisel the end and then sand it to make a rounded end for pushing into soil.

A GARDEN FORK: This has shorter and fatter prongs than a manure fork producing better durability for jobs like digging out plants, including parsnips, and for removing perennial weeds such as couch grass. Look for a sturdy handle that won't snap at the first hint of something firm.

A MANURE FORK: For turning and spreading compost and organic matter generally. Long, thin prongs make it too weak for any kind of digging work.

A HOE: Ensure it has a thin blade and a sharp edge that slides easily through soil. The aim is to cut through all roots of small weeds at a shallow level, without bringing up lumps of soil in which they might survive before withering. Hoes come in many forms: Dutch hoes, draw hoes, onion hoes and swivel hoes, all with blades of varied size and at different angles. I recommend trying a few to see which you like, because everybody has a favourite type. I use a copper swivel hoe: its thin, sharp blade cuts cleanly when both pushing and pulling.

A RAKE: A standard, short-pronged rake is handy before sowing seeds, to knock lumps apart and create a smoother tilth, and to fill drills after sowing; also for collecting up surface debris such as leaves and grass.

A POCKET KNIFE: This is often needed for cutting string, sticks and flowers, trimming leeks, cabbages and tomato plants, deadheading and many of the other jobs that catch one's eye unexpectedly. It is a good habit to carry one in the pocket.

A TROWEL: This is more useful than any other tool, for clearing ground, removing perennial weeds and making holes to plant tomatoes, courgettes and potatoes. Copper trowels are the easiest to use: they retain a sharp edge and slide easily through soil.

A SPADE: Even in a no-dig garden a spade is useful for making holes for trees and large plants, shaping beds, chopping waste matter, and digging parsnips. A sharp end is invaluable. Copper or stainless-steel spades are worth the extra money.

A WATERING CAN: This is vital for watering in dry periods. Choose as large a can as is comfortable to hold when full. A smaller can with a fine rose is useful for propagating plants.

A WHEELBARROW: The barrow ranks with the bicycle as a supremely cost-effective, energy-efficient and useful invention for carrying all kinds of materials, to and from the compost heap above all.

A thin weak handle makes the steel trowel vulnerable to pressure.

A few accessories

Many accessories are cheap for the benefits they bring: fleece is easy to use and cost effective, and though polytunnels may seem daunting to erect they offer wonderful new ways of achieving better harvests.

Good to have

A CLOCHE: For growing salads in winter, and for warming the air and soil in spring. Covering hoops with polythene affords most warmth to plants but means some ventilation and watering are often needed. Alternatively you can lay fleece or mesh over cloche hoops, ensuring good ventilation or, more simply, directly on to plants.

A COLD FRAME: For starting seedlings and protecting tender plants. Glass is best for slug-free growth.

A COMPOST BIN: One with wooden sides or a simple enclosure of old pallets is effective. Plastic bins are reliable too.

A SELECTION OF CONTAINERS: Use anything that can hold compost and has a drainage hole at the bottom. Terracotta pots need more water than plastic. You can grow in boxes or crates that have been used for packing food; line any with holes with newspaper.

FLEECE & MESH: These are reusable and offer weather protection. Fleece is warmer than mesh and is invaluable in spring, for covering young plants, also as a pest barrier in summer and autumn, and, doubled, as frost protection in winter. For protection against aphids and midges you need the finest grade mesh.

NETTING: For protection against pigeons, deer and rabbits. Mesh size starts from 2.5cm (1in). I find a 4m (13ft) wide roll of heavy-duty, black netting useful for many crops: its flexible diamond mesh fits different widths of beds, held up by sticks or cloche hoops.

PROPAGATING TRAYS: For indoor sowing and potting on. Seed trays are simple to use but moving plants out of them disturbs seedling roots. With module trays (also called cell or plug trays) you can push plants out with minimal damage.

A SHED: Provides solid shelter for tools and also for storing harvested crops.

A WATER BUTT: Invaluable if there are ways to fill and refill it. Plastic butts of 100–200 litres may have lids and taps, but their water becomes smelly over time. Periodic cleaning is worthwhile.

Compost containers are tidy but may contain rodents too.

JANUARY
weeks 1 & 2

JANUARY
weeks 3 & 4

JANUARY
Jobs for the month

The early weeks of the year are always quiet, and how much needs doing depends on what you achieved in autumn. It should be possible to harvest plants such as leeks and parsnips growing in undug soil covered by a mulch of compost, which freezes less hard than dug soil.

COMPOSTING: Spread well-rotted compost or manure on any bare soil, thus allowing time for frost to soften the organic matter.

RAKING/FORKING: In less cold and drier weather, break open the larger lumps of surface manure and compost that were spread in autumn. This will allow a soft tilth to develop over all the soil.

SOWING: Although it is possible for a few vegetables, there is little to be gained from sowing seeds outdoors now, although garlic can be planted if you have not already done so. You can make indoor sowings of lettuce, spinach, onion, cabbage, cauliflower and broad beans.

HARVESTING: Roots such as parsnip and swede can be lifted – leeks too. If birds and animals can be kept at bay, there can be kale, Brussels sprouts, and cabbages such as 'Tundra' and 'January King'. Gather salad leaves too.

Salad leaves in January from my polytunnel (yellow leaves are chicory forced indoors).

FEBRUARY

FEBRUARY sees greenhouses, conservatories and polytunnels come into their own, for harvests of salads sown in September, and the first sowings of lettuce, spinach, peas and tomatoes under cover. The latter need extra warmth and are best germinated in a heated space first. Outdoors you can still be picking leeks, parsnips, kale and sowing broad beans.

Growing in the space you have

Vegetables need the sunniest position available, far from walls and trees. Start with a small area and crop it well; just one well-managed bed can be more productive than a larger, weedy plot. When starting with a new plot, be prepared to spend extra time clearing and composting weedy ground during the first year, to create clean and fertile soil. This initial expense of time and effort will be repaid many times over in years to come, when you will be sowing and reaping with only light weeding.

What makes an ideal situation?

A perfect site for vegetable growing would enjoy full sunlight and some shelter from wind, with free-draining soil, which also possessed enough body and organic matter to retain moisture in dry spells. Around the edge of this plot might be a clear area of mown grass or hardstanding. Any trees or hedges would not be large enough to shade the growing area, or to suck moisture from it. Ground can be sloping but not so steeply that it is impossible to push a wheelbarrow up it.

Crops for challenging sites

- Trees and hedges can be a difficult issue because their presence is so welcome, except for long shadows and their demands on nearby soil. Small, thin gardens, with more edge than middle, offer difficult conditions for vegetables and need more skill in growing.
- Extremely shady gardens are tricky for sun-loving, summer vegetables such as sweetcorn, courgettes and tomatoes, but salads can work in such sites, slugs permitting. Slugs are a serious problem in damp shade and are often numerous in walls.
- Most enclosed areas receive some sun during summer, so tomatoes may be possible, especially if there is a warm wall to hold the heat and give shelter. Container growing is worth considering, but bear in mind that container-grown vegetables need extra watering and are vulnerable to slugs. Where space is limited, salad plants offer the highest yield of tasty produce.
- If shade is mostly from deciduous trees and shrubs, vegetables that do some of their growing in winter months are worth trying. Oriental salad leaves, land cress, corn salad, purple sprouting broccoli, kale, spring cabbage, garlic and overwintered broad beans should be possible.
- Hard, dense and stony soils can be significantly mitigated by constructing raised beds filled with fertile compost. Concentrating your time and resources on a small area is best: start with just one or two beds of fertile ingredients, in the best part of your site.

New beds in June created in just six months: the whole area was grass and weeds in the previous December.

Raising plants under cover

Starting seeds off under cover is particularly important in a climate such as Britain's, where the growing season is too short for vegetables such as tomato, pepper and aubergine to mature from an outdoor sowing. Early sowing also helps to bring forward the harvest of almost all vegetables, from courgettes, summer beans and beetroot to calabrese and cauliflower, so greatly extending the season.

Where to sow

A windowsill in the house is a convenient place to start seeds, and they often germinate quickly in the ambient heat of the home. However, after the first fortnight or so the levels of light are insufficient to support sturdy growth of the seedlings, so before that they need to go into a space with light from at least three sides, such as a cold frame or shelter attached to a house wall – many garden catalogues sell these.

A larger, walk-in structure such as a greenhouse or polytunnel, fitted with shelving and a small bench to work on, makes an excellent propagating space. You will need containers for sowing and potting on, and a small can with a fine rose for watering. Other than these basic accessories, there is no need to buy expensive and fancy gadgetry.

Choosing compost

When compost is called 'multipurpose', it can be used for both sowing and potting, but the best success in sowing comes with non-lumpy, free-draining media which have fewer nutrients, so adding sand or vermiculite to a multipurpose compost often helps seeds to germinate better. You often need to remove stones and twigs from compost.

Sowing and watering needs

Different vegetables have varying requirements for moisture and temperature so always check the sowing instructions for particular types of seed.

Many small seeds can be sown into seed trays or small pots for pricking out when they are seedlings. Instead of sowing in a tray you can sow seeds in twos and threes into modules or the smallest-size pots, for thinning to the strongest seedling. Some vegetables, onions and beetroot for example, can be sown five or six seeds in a module or pot and then planted out as clumps of seedlings, without thinning. Larger seeds such as peas, beans and sweetcorn can be sown into trays of larger modules, or small pots of 5cm (2in) diameter.

After filling your seed tray or module container, water the compost thoroughly before sowing, then give only a light sprinkling after. A rule of thumb is to cover seeds with twice as much depth of compost as the seeds are thin (width not length), so most seeds need just a light sprinkling of compost. Seeds of celery, celeriac and lettuce germinate better for having light on them, without any covering of compost; use a sheet of glass over a seed tray instead.

Will you need a heated unit?

Heat is usually not necessary except for frost-susceptible plants on cold nights between March and early May. Laying fleece and/or bubble wrap on such plants at night when frost is expected is often sufficient protection, but in larger structures it is useful to have an electrically heated propagation bench or heating mats.

Watering

Be careful to avoid overwatering recently sown seeds and small seedlings. Seeds sown in fully moistened compost need only occasional, light sprinklings until after their first true leaves are visible. As seedlings grow their need for water increases steadily, especially in sunny weather, so be aware of the weather forecast and water accordingly. Water in the morning, so that plants are not cooled and left damp after watering in the evening, which can cause mildew on leaves and make it easier for slugs to install overnight.

Pests in propagation

Keep propagating areas clean and tidy and avoid providing damp habitats for slugs; just one slug can destroy whole batches of seedlings. Should slug damage occur, hunt for the culprits under seed and module trays, and scan the area with a torch after dark. Woodlice nibble leaves and stems, particularly of spinach, tomato and cucumber. The best precaution is to thoroughly clean and sweep the propagating area before you make any sowings. Mice often appear out of nowhere when peas, beans and sweetcorn are sown and I find it wise to set a mousetrap when sowing larger seeds.

Diseases

The most common is damping off, when small seedlings fall over and then rot, usually at cotyledon (two-leaf) stage. It is caused mainly by too much moisture. Avoid it by sowing thinly, watering seeds and seedlings infrequently and by using free-draining seed compost, especially for lettuce and basil. Take care to sow seeds in their correct season.

Greenhouse sowings of spinach, lettuce, onion, pea, beetroot, cabbage and tree spinach.

FEBRUARY
weeks 1 & 2

Why no-dig?

I have run a no-dig experiment since 2007 in order to understand the effect on soil of digging and not digging. In it I compare growth of the same vegetables growing side by side in dug and undug beds.

In the absence of digging, I have found that harvests are as high, sometimes higher, while some extra quality of growth on undug soil may be apparent. Soil in the undug beds, with compost on its surface, is well drained, retains more moisture in dry springs and grows fewer weeds and stronger vegetables, especially at the start of the season.

A key point is that undug soil is firm. This is a desirable state and not at all the same as compacted soil. Roots have freedom to travel, at the same time as being well anchored.

Fertility is enhanced by an increase of undisturbed soil life, which mobilizes nutrients and helps plant roots to access them. This is most noticeable in early spring, when growth on undug soil is generally faster by comparison with dug soil, whose fertility, in terms of soil life, is still recovering from the winter digging.

Setting up the experiment

In March 2007 I laid four wooden frames of 1.5 x 2.5m (5 x 8ft) on the grass and weeds of a clay-soil pasture.

I filled the two undug beds with 20cm (8in) of compost, which I placed on top of the grass, dandelions and buttercups. One-third of this compost was well-rotted

The experiment in May 2011: undug bed in front, dug bed behind.

horse manure as a first layer; then I used green waste compost for the remaining two-thirds and 10kg (22lb) of rockdust. All sowing and planting on the undug beds is into the surface compost.

I created the two dug beds by first lifting turves off the pasture, and then placing the same ingredients as in the undug beds in the holes created, finally putting the upside-down turves on top.

Running the experiment

I fed and cropped the four beds as two pairs, giving each pair the same ingredients, except that I either put compost and/or manure on top (undug) or incorporated them (dug). I re-dug the dug beds every December, when I gave both beds a barrowload of either home-made compost or well-rotted animal manure, equivalent to about a 5cm (2in) layer.

I sowed or planted each pair of beds with identical crops and I replaced any eaten plants and sowings to equalize the harvests aspect of the experiment; failed sowings, fortunately, were rare. I harvested at the same time, weighing and recording crops, together with any observations on differences in quality.

Harvests from the experiment

Yields in both beds were excellent, thanks to timely planting and replanting, good amounts of organic matter and moisture-retentive, clay soil. Over a whole season, each bed produced about 30kg (66lb) of vegetables. The table shows harvests of six years (2007–12), comparing those of dug and undug beds.

The differences between early and late harvests show how the no-dig beds start growing more quickly in spring, and the dug beds catch up in late summer and autumn.

Differences in growth

Discrepancies in growth on dug and undug beds were most apparent between March and June, when the dug soil, it seems, was recovering from being turned over and broken up. During spring and early summer, many vegetables on the dug beds, especially radish, onions and spinach, started growing more slowly. I also noticed that in the undug beds the leaves of spinach and lettuce were thicker and glossier, the radish roots were shinier and the onions had a deeper colour.

Then from about July there was a change as growth on the dug soil speeded up: celeriac on the dug beds, for instance, which was smaller in June, suddenly grew faster from July, and by October had more or less caught up with celeriac on the undug soil. Summer-planted brassicas sometimes yielded better on the dug beds.

Differences in surfaces

It is fascinating to compare the smooth, brown clay of the dug soil with the fluffy, darker compost of the undug. When watering in dry spells, I am struck by how easily the fast-flowing hose water soaks into the undug beds, being absorbed by the surface compost and then passing downwards through the unbroken capillary channels of the soil below. By contrast on the dug beds the water tends to cause a smearing of clay and then runs downhill before it can all soak in, so I have to apply it in short bursts. Thankfully I find that by late summer it is easier to water the dug soil, which suggests that soil organisms have, by then, restructured their home.

The results

The table of harvests shows much variation between vegetables; this is partly because of their season and partly because of their family. Digging damages mycorrhizal fungi in the soil, which work with the roots of many plants to help them source nutrients. Plant roots of the brassica family are thought not to use mycorrhizal allies to improve their rooting, which probably explains the bigger harvests of cabbage and turnip on dug, but kale bucked this trend.

VEGETABLE	HARVEST FROM TWO BEDS DUG kg***	HARVEST FROM TWO BEDS UNDUG kg***
Beans, dwarf 6 years	8.38	7.76
Beetroot 6 years*	15.55	18.01
Cabbage, red/white 4 years*	12.29	8.87
Calabrese 1 year	1.12	0.62
Carrots 5 years*	13.34	16.52
Celeriac 5 years	21.18	24.42
Chard 2 years*	12.33	11.59
Endive & chicory 5 years	16.45	19.07
Kale 5 years	10.90	11.81
Leek 5 years	16.68	18.47
Lettuce 6 years*	51.17	55.07
Onion 6 years*	36.06	40.07
Peas Tall Sugar 5 years*	41.03	40.86
Parsnip 5 years	56.10	57.68
Potatoes, early 5 years*	18.46	17.64
Radish 4 years*	2.37	2.92
Salads, autumn 5 years	5.71	7.36
Spinach 5 years*	23.09	29.34
Turnip, radish 4 years	14.03	12.30
TOTAL	376.24	400.38
Early harvests*	225.69	240.89
Late harvests**	150.55	159.49

* Early harvests are from April to early August and include beetroot, chard, lettuce, onion, peas, potatoes, radish and spinach.   ** Late harvests are all other vegetables listed here.   ***1kg equals 2.2lb.

How no-dig works

Air is a vital ingredient of soil, but think of the soil underneath a lawn or a field of grazing animals, where the grass grows in spite of being walked and trodden on. This is because of an enduring structure of air channels in the soil, held in place by aggregations of organic matter and plant roots.

Soil for vegetable growing can be the same, but it does not have the roots of perennially present plants. We need to replace the structure these afford by adding organic matter to feed all the bacteria, fungi, nematodes and worms, helping them to maintain an open soil. They create soil structure far better than we can with tools and machinery.

Firm soil or compacted soil?

Soil in a normal, firm, open state is often wrongly labelled as 'compacted soil'. Put another way, 'open' is not the same as 'fluffy'. Soil that has been mechanically loosened and fluffed up is not in a stable state; hence the need to walk on planks after digging heavy soil, to avoid compaction. By contrast, it is actually difficult to compact a healthy, undug soil.

True soil compaction

Compaction is caused by a combination of heavy pressure, moisture, soil disturbance and a lack of both organic matter and growing roots: for example, in over-cultivated fields and gardens during wet weather, especially just after cultivation, and on fields or building sites where big machines are passing on wet soil.

Compacted soil is squishy when wet, rock-like when dry and more dead than alive. It contains few or no worm channels, is difficult to crumble in your hand and may smell sulphurous because of a lack of oxygen. Man-made compaction occurs mostly near the surface, in the top 15–20cm (6–8in), which should be possible to check with a spade. Compacted clay discolours, turning a dull grey or orange. If you see any of these signs, you need to add plenty of organic matter to the soil and then be patient while it enables life to return.

What is 'fertility'?

Soil fertility is often presented as a sufficiency of nutrients, meaning that there is enough food for plants, but this is just part of the story. The other part is soil life: the presence of enough organisms both to make nutrients available, as when soil inhabitants die and are recycled into food, and to help plant roots feed on these nutrients.

Mycorrhizal fungi are a good example of biological fertility. In cooperation with many plants, their almost invisible filaments are able to travel long distances in search of nutrients needed by plants, which roots can then use. In return, the fungi are fed by carbohydrates travelling back down the roots, a product of photosynthesis by plants' leaves. So plants are fed and the fungi are fed, in an arrangement of mutual help called symbiosis.

If soil is cultivated, these beneficial fungi mostly die from being physically broken up and from being exposed to air and drying winds. Their need to recover, which my experiment suggests takes six to eight months, is a factor in some plants on dug soil being slower growing than those on undug beds, and sometimes then catching up later in the season.

Life in the soil

In healthy soil there are huge numbers of a vast range of inhabitants, of all sizes, from microscopic bacteria and fungi to beetles and toads. They all have roles, and their roles all overlap and depend on others.

I suggest that leaving them all in peace is the kindest approach and most beneficial to us, since our plants can then grow better as a result of their undisturbed labours.

Feeding the soil

Gardening becomes simple when the main emphasis is on looking after soil. Fertile soil can cater for the needs of a vast range of healthy plants, in all seasons, without the gardener needing to worry about the various requirements of each one.

For example, I often read advice to make a deep trench of organic matter before planting climbing beans. In fact you can avoid this huge amount of work and simply plant beans into surface-composted soil.

This soil is compacted clay that has become orange and grey from lack of air.

This is dense but open undug clay soil, with many plant roots, air channels and a worm!

FEBRUARY
weeks 3 & 4

FEBRUARY
Jobs for the month

February is a quiet time in the garden, and the weather will often dictate how much can be done outside. There should still be plenty of winter crops to harvest this month.

COMPOSTING: Continue to spread well-rotted compost on bare soil, and rake or fork over surface manure and compost that was spread earlier, knocking any lumps open.

SOWING: In many places it is still too cold and wet for most vegetables to be sown outside, but if it is dry enough parsley, dill, parsnips and broad beans can be sown after mid-month. Indoors sow broad beans, cabbage, cauliflower, lettuce and spinach. Parsley can also be sown inside, perhaps in a pot on a windowsill.

HARVESTING: Continue to lift root crops and leeks. Undug soil that has been well mulched with compost does not freeze as hard as dug soil, making winter roots and leeks easier to harvest in cold spells. There should still be winter greens such as kale, Brussels sprouts and hardy cabbages. If the weather is reasonably mild, towards the second half of the month it should be possible to harvest a few salad leaves under cover and some lamb's lettuce outside. February salad leaves look less perfect but their taste is rich.

Six September-sown mustard plants in a box in February: (left to right) 'Green in the Snow', 'Red Frills' and 'Pizzo'.

MARCH

Any dry days in MARCH, even
if cold, can be spent making
more beds, doing some weeding
with your new year resolution
to be on top of weeds, and
using a rake or fork lightly
to knock out larger lumps of
compost and manure on the soil
surface. Many indoor sowings
are possible of tomatoes,
spinach and leeks amongst
others, but wait until mild
days before sowing outdoors.

Sowing outside

It is important to give yourself the best chance of success by sowing individual crops according to their needs – for instance, by making sure you sow courgettes and summer beans at a time and in a place of sufficient warmth. This will lead to stronger, healthier growth.

Harvesting time also represents a key part of deciding when to sow. Leaf vegetables have most flexibility in sowing dates, according to when you want them to produce, compared to fruit and some root vegetables, which are generally date specific, especially those that need a whole season to ripen their fruit or grow their roots.

Temperatures for sowing

By dividing the most grown, temperate-clime vegetables into bands of temperature, according to their seeds' requirements for good germination and growth, it turns out that many in the cool category are grown for harvests of leaves, while many in the medium category are vegetables grown for roots. Vegetables grown for fruits and seeds such as aubergine, French and runner beans, courgette, cucumber, pepper, pumpkin, squash, sweetcorn and tomato tend to need warmer conditions (18–30°C/ 64–86°F), and are raised under cover rather than being sown direct outdoors.

Almost all seeds in the cool and medium categories of vegetables will germinate and grow at warmer temperatures, but warm-category seeds would struggle to grow in cooler temperatures, except after being germinated in a warm place such as an airing cupboard.

Sow direct

Many vegetables are sown directly where they are to mature, and the seedlings are thinned as necessary.

For small seeds such as carrots draw drills to a depth of 1–2.5cm ($1/2$–1in) in surface soil or compost, and sow about twice as many seeds as you want plants, so that after thinning the plants will be at the spacings indicated on the packaging. For larger seeds such as peas and beans, dib holes at the recommended spacings and depths. When sown outdoors seeds need to be placed deeper than when sown in modules.

POSSIBLE SOWING TEMPERATURES	
Cool (5–12°C/41–54°F)	Brassicas, broad bean, carrot, lettuce, parsnip, peas, radish, sorrel, spinach
Medium (10–20°C/50–68°F	Beetroot, celeriac, celery, chard, chervil, chicory, coriander, endive, fennel for bulb, onion, parsley, swede

Sow and transplant

Some vegetables are sown in 'nursery beds' outside and the young plants that develop are then lifted and transplanted to where they are to mature.

To raise plants outside, draw drills as for sowing direct and sow seeds more thickly, every 1cm ($\frac{1}{2}$in), to grow a row with plenty of plants for setting out elsewhere. If making more than one drill, space them 25–30cm (10–12in) apart.

Vegetables to sow outdoors in March

BROCCOLI (CALABRESE) & CAULIFLOWER: Sow March–June, transplant April–July for heads in summer and autumn. March and April sowings are at less risk of caterpillar damage than plants sown in May.

CARROTS: For early carrots sow late March–April, 2–3 seeds per cm (5–7 per inch) in rows of 30cm (12in). Thin after a month to one seedling per 1cm ($\frac{1}{2}$in).

LETTUCE FOR HEARTS & LEAVES: Outdoor sowings need covering with soil, but only a little, and watering every five days or so in dry weather. After 4–6 weeks, plants can be thinned when they are still small but perhaps large enough to eat.

ONIONS FOR SALAD: Expect to do some careful weeding around the slow-growing seedlings. Make sure you use fresh seed.

PARSLEY: Parsley germinates and grows slowly at first, especially in early spring. Flat-leaved parsley germinates and grows a little more quickly than curly-leaved, but also flowers more readily, so it is a good idea to sow some of each seed.

PARSNIP: Can be sown as early as February but slightly later sowings are more reliable. Parsnip seed is slow to germinate and it helps to sow a few radish seeds in the drill with it, because the radishes' fast growth allows you to see the line where parsnip seedlings will emerge.

PEAS FOR SHOOTS: Once you have mastered the knack of picking them, pea shoots become an easy and delicious addition to salads. Peas are hardy and survive frost and snow, but fleece helps them to establish more quickly. Choose seed of a tall-growing variety (to 2m/6ft) so that shoots are longer and more vigorous.

RADISH: For a spring and early summer harvest sow now. Thin after a month to 1 x 25cm ($\frac{1}{2}$ x 10in).

SORREL, BROAD-LEAVED: Sorrel, which has tiny seeds, is a perennial, and one sowing may give you plants that survive many years.

SPINACH: When spinach is sown in early spring, the plants have time to make plenty of leaf before their summer flowering.

Grown in undug soil, I harvested these March-sown parsnips in November.

What kind of beds?

When creating beds, it is often assumed that some kinds of wooden or plastic sides are needed, but this is not so because vegetables grow well on beds without sides and also on level ground. Sides are most useful when you want to increase fertility and rooting depth in a smaller and defined area.

Beds with sides

ADVANTAGES

- Where space is limited, raised beds yield more vegetables because of their depth of growing medium – preferably plenty of good compost.
- They reduce the amount of bending downwards needed and can be raised higher for those who have trouble reaching down.
- Such beds offer a clear definition of growing areas, which is useful when plots are shared.
- Just one or two beds are an excellent way for beginners to learn vegetable growing.
- Paths in between may be mulched with membrane, wood chips or gravel, meaning no dirty feet.

DISADVANTAGES

- The cost of materials with which to create and fill raised beds, and the time needed for this.
- Some extra watering is required, especially for beds with wooden and high sides.
- Slugs and woodlice may inhabit the spaces between sides and the bed, causing problems with seedlings and small plants.

Beds without sides

Not having sides and ends avoids much time and expense. This method is especially suitable for larger plots and allotments, and works well in my gardens. Comparing growth of vegetables on these beds with a handful of wooden-sided beds, I notice little difference, except for less slug and woodlice damage in open beds.

The advantages are much the same as for beds with sides. A major difference is that beds are less raised, especially by late spring when hungry birds are looking for worms in the surface compost, kicking some of it into pathways. This actually helps to keep the paths fertile and well structured for walking on.

Also, beds that are less high conserve more moisture. The profile of beds in my garden is gently undulating rather than one of horizontals and verticals.

Growing on level ground

Having no beds, marking out rows as needed and then walking between them is a third way, which often follows the digging of a whole plot, when all trace of previous rows and paths is lost: widely spaced vegetables such as potatoes and Brussels sprouts are suitable for this approach. However, the emphasis of this book is towards growing higher-value vegetables in a more intensive way, and this is most effective in beds.

Keeping paths weed-free

Paths

Paths offer as much chance to be creative as the beds they surround. I suggest a width between adjacent beds of 45cm (18in), for general access, and a little wider for beds with sides if a wheelbarrow is to pass between.

PATHS FOR BEDS WITHOUT SIDES:

Weeds are an issue for many pathways. The golden rule with paths, as much as with beds, is to clean them in the first year with light-excluding mulch, as described on page 162. If you allow perennial weeds such as couch grass to grow in paths, they will gradually colonize the adjacent beds.

Once the path soil is clean, I find it good to cover it, just once, with 5cm (2in) of basic compost such as green waste or composted bark, as long as it can be

sourced cheaply. These composts are weed free, make weeding and hoeing easier, and improve the path's fertility, which benefits the vegetables growing in beds on either side. A once-only mulching and composting of paths is enough; then just keep them clean at all times.

I do not recommend gravel for paths, because it ultimately gets mixed into the soil, chiefly through worms casting above it. It may look pretty and discourage slugs for a while, but eventually you have a gravely soil, for ever, unless you also use a plastic membrane under the gravel, in which roots become entangled. I have similar reservations about wood chips and feel there is a danger of over-elaborating path coverings.

Other possibilities include leaves, straw and cardboard or paper, whose mulching properties will keep weeds down and conserve moisture. But light-excluding mulches afford shelter for slugs, whereas compost does not.

PATHS FOR BEDS WITH SIDES: There

are more options for paths of beds with sides because wooden sides are an effective barrier to the passage of annual plants, so it is feasible to have grass, for instance, as long as it is kept short. However, perennial weeds can still be invasive, especially if you do not regularly cut the paths.

I suggest a general mulch before creating beds, to clear all weeds. Then mulch paths between the beds with compost, wood chips or bark, and hoe or pull out all weeds you see.

First summer after grass, with cardboard on paths to weaken couch grass.

Dealing
with weeds

Weeds are plants that we do not want because they take light, water and food from our vegetables. Most soil is full of weed seeds and roots, with germination of weed seeds triggered by their exposure to light. Dormant seeds also germinate in response to changes in temperature and moisture. Perennial weeds mostly grow from roots lurking in the soil, sometimes unsuspected until the growing season. This all results in different weeds through the year, with never a dull moment!

Weeds are soil's way of keeping itself covered, of recycling nutrients, of increasing organic matter and also, I have come to suspect, of recovering an equilibrium that is disturbed by cultivation.

Where weeds thrive

Fewer weeds germinate on undug soil because there is no need for it to recover, in the sense of recovering from cultivation. And the cover of a compost mulch seems to replicate, in part at least, the cover of growing plants. Surface-composted undug soil therefore grows fewer weeds than dug soil with compost incorporated.

However, some weed seeds blow in, and others arrive with dressings of compost and manure. I usually find a flush of new weed seedlings in spring, but they are easy to hoe or pull out of the friable compost, when still small.

As well as the fact that weeds compete with our vegetables for light, water and food, there is another equally important and often overlooked reason to keep on top of weeds. Weeds are extremely fast and efficient at reproducing themselves, either by root or by seed, and this leads to difficulties

with the next sowings and plantings. For example, your onions have grown well and are bulbing up in early July. At this stage, their growth is not hampered by the weeds growing around them, and one could say that it is actually better for the soil to be covered. It may also be the case that some other plants growing near the onions help them to ripen by depriving them of too many nutrients, especially nitrogen.

However, allowing weeds to grow is extremely risky. If you leave the onions unweeded during their last few weeks, by the time you pull the onions in August, some weeds that have been allowed to grow will have set seed and others will have developed strong roots, so that they can't simply be pulled out, let alone hoed off, especially in a wet summer. Then it becomes a major task to grow more vegetables in that space, such as sowings of turnip and endive or a planting of bulb fennel, unless you spend a lot of time clearing the soil.

Little and often

Instead of the above, what if you pull the small weed seedlings emerging among the onions as they mature in July? This takes much less time in the end, because small plants pull out so much more easily than large ones. Two quick weedings in July will keep the ground clean, and you can quickly pull any weed seedlings in early August when you harvest the onions.

Then, in the clean soil, it is simple to draw a drill for seeds of turnip, endive, rocket and oriental salad leaves, or to dib holes for plants of late calabrese, bulb fennel and radicchio, and subsequently to continue with occasional small amounts of weeding until season's end. By that time you will have enjoyed a second harvest; the soil will still be clean, ready for some compost, and you can look forward to next year without dread of new sowings being engulfed by weeds.

How much weeding?

Once your initial clearances and mulching have cleaned the soil of perennial weed roots, most subsequent weeding will be of small, newly germinated weed seedlings. How many weed seeds germinate will depend partly on whether you dug or mulched to remove any perennials.

After digging there will be a relative explosion of weed seedlings, and hoeing is the quickest way to deal with them.

After mulching to remove perennial weeds, and especially in soil that has a thin covering of mostly weed-free compost and manure on top, few new weeds will grow and much less weeding will be needed – just a small weeding every fortnight or so.

Weeds and grass can be mulched with any combination of manure, compost, cardboard, polythene and membranes, without disturbing soil underneath.

TIP: I recommend you also search for new weeds under the leaves of spreading vegetables such as calabrese and squashes, to avoid any growing large enough to flower and seed while out of sight.

How to grow:
TOMATOES

Growing tomatoes at home allows you to choose from an exciting range of flavours, colours and fruit size. In Britain, however, an outdoor harvest is rarely assured, because tomatoes need warmth, a long season of growth, and dry leaves if blight is not to be a problem. For wetter areas in the north and west, I suggest growing tomatoes under cover. In a polytunnel they can usefully follow on from winter salad crops.

WHERE & WHEN TO SOW: Sow indoors in warmth (20–30°C/ 68–86°F) in late February or March, first in a seed tray or small modules; then pot on the plants after a month or so.

WHEN TO PLANT & SPACING: May for indoor planting; early June for outdoor planting. Space plants at a minimum of 45cm (18in): 60cm (24in) allows better growth and more room to pick fruit, remove weeds and prune plants.

CARE: Plants should be 20–30cm (8–12in) high at planting time. It is good if they have their first truss of flower buds just developing as they are planted. Avoid planting too early in case an unexpected spring frost kills the plants – they need warm weather to grow well.

TIP: Less water is needed by September and you can stop watering indoors altogether from mid-September, to encourage ripening and increase the sweetness of the tomatoes.

'Sungold' tomatoes in a polytunnel in September, grown in soil that was manured but not fed.

Tomato types

First decide which kind and size of plant to grow:

- a bush variety at soil level;
- a tumbling variety for hanging baskets;
- a determinate (cordon) variety for staking and training, up to 2m (7ft).

Then have a look at all the fruit options – cherry for sweetness, plum for cooking, normal size for yield, or beef for texture and flavour. I suggest in a first year of growing tomatoes that you buy one plant each of many different varieties to try them out, rather than sowing lots of seeds all the same.

The soil for tomatoes must be rich and moisture retentive. A 5–7cm (2–3in) dressing of animal manure can provide enough nutrients for sustained growth, without any liquid feeding. I water twice weekly in hot weather, but containers often need daily watering in sunny weather and when plants are large. Try to keep water off the leaves.

Support is needed for cordon plants: either a cane or stout stick, with plant stems tied loosely to it at intervals of about 20cm (8in). Or in polytunnels use string, with one end placed in the planting hole when planting, where it will become held securely in the soil by tomato roots enveloping it. Tie the top of the string to the structure above and twist the plants around it as they grow.

Cordon plants need side shooting at planting time and weekly thereafter: remove each new stem (shoot) that grows out of the main stem, just above where each main leaf joins the main stem. Cordons need their main growing point removed in August, to encourage ripening of existing fruit rather than formation of more young tomatoes. Likewise, pinch

Growing in containers

Bush or trailing types are excellent in containers. Cordon tomatoes can be grown in large containers or growbags, and need weekly feeding from July to September and almost daily watering.

out all growing points of bush tomatoes through August and September.

Cropping starts from late June indoors, for early varieties such as 'Sungold', and continues until October, when all remaining, fully grown fruit are best picked to finish ripening in the warmth of a house. Tomatoes taste best when at least three-quarters coloured; later they are a little bland.

Possible problems

Blight is the number one problem – for more detail see page 133.

Nematodes in soil that has grown tomatoes for several years can hamper growth, but plants will fruit well nonetheless. After experimenting with expensive, grafted plants that boast resistance to nematodes, I feel that soil pests pose less of a threat than sometimes suggested, unless you are a commercial grower of long-season tomatoes every year. Also I find that the exuberant growth of grafted plants can delay ripening of fruit.

Seed freshness

When it comes to buying seed, there are plenty of choices, but of variable quality. A particular problem is that when we buy seed we have no way of knowing its age. Sometimes this is unimportant, but in cases when it matters, especially parsnip and beets, whole sowings, much time and even an entire harvest can be lost. This has happened to me more often than I would like.

I have asked many in the seed trade for assurances on seed freshness, not always successfully, and have experienced poor germination of seed from no fewer than seven of the companies I buy from, in trials comparing their seed with other batches. When informed, they reply that germination was above the mandatory level when the seeds were last tested.

However, there is a clear difference between the 'germination' of a seed radicle – the first shoot to grow out of the seed – whose growth may subsequently peter out, and normal growth of the kind we need in our gardens. The latter happens when seed is reasonably fresh, although some vegetables seed can be viable when older.

The figures given in the table are the longest recommended time for keeping seed, from their time of harvest. Numbers are based partly on my experience and partly on the advice of the seed company Real Seeds.

A difficulty is that these figures mask the main problem of bought seed: we know only its date of purchase and packaging, rather than its date of harvest, which would have been at least a year earlier. After saving some seed, sow it alongside some bought seed to compare the growth.

HOW LONG CAN YOU KEEP SEED?	
Beans	3–5 years
Beets and chard	2 years; older seed grows more slowly
Cabbage family	3–7 years
Carrot	2–3 years
Courgette, squash	2–3 years; older seed is almost useless
Cucumber, melon	6–8 years
Lettuce	2–4 years; a marked decline in vigour after two years
Onion, salad onion, leek	2 years; then viability declines quickly
Parsnip	1–2 years
Peas	at least 4 years, possibly longer
Pepper, aubergine	3 years
Tomato	5–8 years

TIP: Seed needs to be kept in a dry state. Coolness helps too, but dry is the most important factor. Home-saved seed keeps well in old envelopes or food containers; avoid polythene bags which trap any residual moisture.

MARCH
week 1

MARCH
week 2

How to grow: SPINACH

WHERE & WHEN TO SOW: Sow direct March–April and then July, or indoors February–April and then late July.

SPACING: 15–22cm (6–9in) apart.

CARE: There are two good periods for sowing spinach: early spring; and late summer (for plants to stand the winter).

Spinach grows equally well from direct or indoor sowings; the latter are easier to keep free of nibbles by slugs, birds and woodlice. Sow three or four seeds per module or small pot and plant as a clump.

Spinach sown in March or April will flower within 2–3 months. It can be cleared by June and followed by many summer and autumn vegetables.

When sown in late July or early August spinach can live for nine months, giving leaves in autumn, surviving the winter and then providing leaves again until the end of May. Spinach is impressively resistant to frost. Be ready for a few slug holes in the leaves during autumn; the flavour of the leaves should compensate for any ragged looks.

Leaf miners can be a nuisance, but I put up with them. Their eating is visible as pale yellow patches in otherwise healthy leaves.

Tree spinach

Tree spinach is an annual, best sown from February indoors to April outside. The tiny seeds grow into 1.5m (5ft) plants by the end of summer, and with harvestable shoots by May or June when plants are 15–20cm high (6–8in). Pinch off the magenta-coloured growing point and then you can pinch off any other pretty side shoots – with just four or six baby leaves on each – on a regular basis; they have little flavour but look gorgeous, and new shoots keep appearing until early September. One plant is enough for abundant harvests, and larger leaves can be cooked.

Spinach is sown in March to give lots of tender pickings by May.

Tree spinach has tender, colourful shoots that can be picked frequently for salad.

How to grow:
LEEKS

WHERE & WHEN TO SOW: Sow outdoors April or indoors March–April.

TIME FROM SOWING TO PLANTING: 5 weeks (indoors) and 8–10 weeks (outdoors).

WHEN TO PLANT & SPACING: May–mid-July, 15cm (6in) or 10 x 30cm (4 x 12in).

CARE: Sow either in modules indoors from March, or around the middle of April in clean, fertile soil outdoors. Clean soil is important because seedling growth is slow and baby leeks have fine, grass-like leaves that allow enough light to pass through for weed growth underneath. The soil needs plenty of organic matter, especially for moisture retention. Summer warmth and moisture enable rapid growth; it is worth watering from July to September if soil becomes dry.

Weeding needs to be little and frequent, because leeks do not cover the soil and some weeds always grow. They are best removed when small.

Cropping starts in August for leeks of early, long-stemmed varieties such as 'Swiss Giant' and 'King Richard', and continues until early May for the most frost-resistant, shorter varieties with darker leaves, such as 'Apollo', 'Bandit', 'Edison' and 'St Victor'. After a dormant period in winter leeks grow again quite fast, until they start to flower in May.

The faster-growing, long-stemmed summer varieties are vulnerable to frosts of about −4°C/25°F or colder, while those for overwintering are shorter and more hardy, finally reaching a good size in March and April.

Growing leeks used to be straightforward until the leek moth became common. If you still don't suffer from it, count your blessings and enjoy harvesting a vegetable that resists slugs and frost and can be eaten from August to May.

'Swiss Giant' leeks planted out in June.

TIP: When planting leeks, use a dibber to make deep, individual holes for each plant and set plants with their roots 7–10cm (3–4in) deep, so that the lower part of the stem will be covered with soil and become white and sweeter. Knock some surface soil or compost back into the holes on top of the leek roots, and water gently so that the plants don't float out.

MARCH
week 3

MARCH
week 4

MARCH
Jobs for the month

Weeds are starting to flourish. By now there will be grasses, chickweed and bittercress to pull, and a trowel is useful for removing roots of dandelion, couch grass and other perennials, which will now be revealing themselves. In a dry spring, hoeing the seedlings of annual weeds is worthwhile.

COMPOSTING: Spread well-rotted compost or manure on any bare soil, thus allowing time for frost to soften the organic matter.

RAKING/FORKING: Break down the remaining lumps of surface manure and compost that were spread in autumn.

SOWING: Indoors as for February and also tomato, chilli, aubergine, pepper, melon (all with some extra warmth),

peas, calabrese, celery, celeriac, beetroot; outdoors parsnip, onion, radish.

PLANTING: Garlic in early March, early potato, onion sets, shallots, broad beans and asparagus crowns after mid-month.

HARVESTING: As for February, but with hints of abundance to come from salad leaves and spinach under cover, purple sprouting broccoli and longer rhubarb stems with each harvest.

I explain how the indoor winter salad plants, seen here in March, have all survived being frozen many times.

APRIL

APRIL can still be cold;
therefore sow only seeds of
plants that tolerate frost. Cover
newly sown and planted areas
with fleece *laid directly on
top* to protect plants from
wind – lay a few stones along
its edges to ensure it does not
blow away. I did this with
lettuce planted 1 April and was
picking leaves within three
weeks, despite continual frost
and wind. Purple sprouting
broccoli and rhubarb are fully
in season now.

APRIL
week 1

Pricking out

Pricking out means the transplanting of small seedlings, sometimes tiny ones. It is something of a lost art and deserves to be well learnt and adopted.

When seeds are sown by being scattered over the surface of compost in trays or pots, the seedlings may come up quite thickly, and if left too long they will soon become overcrowded. This can lead to problems with damping off disease, as well as the seedlings having to compete for their share of light, food and water. Pricking out allows each seedling to be given its own space, so that it can develop properly.

When to prick out

Pricking out is easier with tiny seedlings than small plants. The cotyledon stage is ideal, before any true leaf is visible, and the only tool you require is a pencil.

How to prick out

Use the pencil to 'dig' into the compost near the seedlings, and then underneath their roots, and lift them up in a clump to start with. Then tease them apart, holding them by a leaf, because leaves resist squashing much better than stems.

Seedlings can be put into module trays or small pots (no more than 5cm/2in diameter) filled with well-firmed compost that has already been watered to full or nearly full moisture capacity. Use the pencil to make quite deep, individual holes in each cell or pot, for as many seedlings as you want plants, discarding any weak or noticeably smaller ones. Holding them by their leaves, place

each seedling into a hole so that all its stem is covered with compost and only the leaves are visible. This makes sturdy plants, which can send new roots off the buried stems.

Prick out a few more seedlings than you are likely to need for planting, in case of failures, and then compost unwanted seedlings, because there is no point in raising many more plants than you have room for.

Finally, lightly water the pricked-out seedlings. Then they often won't need water for a day or two afterwards, when they spend time settling in rather than growing.

Pricking out lettuce into holes made by a pencil.

Examples of common perennial weeds

Perennial weeds are more of a nuisance than annual weeds because they are so persistent. This selection will help you identify some of the most common offenders. The times given for each weed are an indication of how long they need covering with a mulch that excludes all light, so that food reserves in their roots are exhausted by continual attempts at regrowing in darkness.

Hedge bindweed

Field bindweed

Bindweed

TIME/EASE OF CLEARING: One year minimum; some regrowth occurs.

Hedge bindweed or bellbind (*Calystegia sepium*) is a vigorous climber with white, trumpet-like flowers and thick, fleshy roots, many of which lie close to the surface. Field bindweed (*Convolvulus arvensis*) has smaller leaves, thinner roots and white or pink flowers that are more discreet.

I have found it possible to eradicate minor infestations of hedge bindweed by persisting for a year, with a combination of using a trowel to lever out any accessible roots, and pulling all its small stems as soon as I see them, to starve roots that cannot be reached.

Field bindweed is less visible but more enduring, and even when frequently pulled or dug out it often spreads in from an edge. An initial mulch is helpful in reducing its vigour, after which I find that infested areas become manageable with frequent but small amounts of trowel work.

Because of bindweed's persistence and longevity, I find it best accepted as a (fading) companion.

Creeping buttercup

(*Ranunculus repens*)
TIME/EASE OF CLEARING: Six months, preferably from late winter to early summer; easy when well covered.

Large amounts of buttercup are hard to remove by digging out because the roots are tenacious, although quite shallow. Mulching is effective within 6–8 months (less in the growing season); subsequent buttercups will grow only from seed and can be hoed.

Creeping buttercup

Couch grass, Quack grass, Twitch
(*Agropyron repens*)
TIME/EASE OF CLEARING: One year; vigorous regrowth from root fragments and invasive from weedy edges.

This weed with spear-like, creeping rhizomes is all too common, often in soil that has been either compacted or over-cultivated at some stage. It responds well, if slowly, to soil enrichment without cultivation and with surface mulching. I have cleared some thick infestations within a year, but two years is more realistic to be completely clear.

Couch grass

Dandelion
(*Taraxacum officinale*)
TIME/EASE OF CLEARING: Six to nine months; remove any weakened survivors with a trowel.

Small numbers can be dug out with a spade: aim to remove 15cm (6in) or more of older roots, so that there is too little left in the soil for viable regrowth. Mulching dandelions works well but takes the best part of a growing season, and is most effective when starting before the end of winter, as soon as leaves are growing again.

Dandelion

Ground elder
(*Aegopodium podagraria*)
TIME/EASE OF CLEARING: One year; some weak regrowth, but this is eradicable.

The roots are tough, medium thick, white and tend to snap as they are being pulled out; use a trowel or fork to follow them as far as possible. They travel horizontally more than vertically and entwine around roots of other plants, making removal difficult except in soil that has no other plants growing in it. In that case, thorough mulching, or digging and extraction of every root fragment, will be effective.

Ground elder

Stinging nettle, Common nettle
(*Urtica dioica*)
TIME/EASE OF CLEARING: Six to nine months; or remove manually. Smaller roots do not regrow.

Nettles are a sign of rich soil and are not too difficult to remove, but wear gloves when handling large plants, using a fork to lever out the main clump of pale yellow roots. Seeding is prolific and seedlings can be hoed.

Stinging nettle

How to grow: POTATOES

Early potatoes are one of the first new vegetables to be ready in June, even in May if late frosts are absent. The flavour of freshly harvested tubers is especially fine and varies interestingly according to variety.

WHERE & WHEN TO PLANT & SPACING: Plant tubers direct, late March–mid-April, 30–40cm (12–16in) apart for first and second earlies; for maincrops plant April–early May, 40–50cm (16–20in) apart.

CARE: Potatoes do not have to be chitted (sprouted), but if you buy tubers a long time before planting them it is worth spreading them in a box near some light, to prevent the growth of long, pale sprouts. Then use a trowel to place tubers 5cm (2in) below soil level.

Potatoes root into firm soil while their tubers need a thick mulch of organic matter. Protect emerging leaves from frost in April and May (cover with pots or earth up as much as possible if frost is forecast). Earth up plants by pulling soil up around the stems as plants grow, to support them and prevent greening of the tubers. Augment the ridging effect by spreading organic matter around plants. If you use unrotted material such as grass and straw, slugs will tend to increase and may damage the tubers. I like to use partly or well-rotted manure and compost, and then level it off after the harvest to grow leeks and autumn salads.

Water is worth giving to large plants when flower buds appear and in dry conditions generally, but avoid continual dampness after mid-June, when blight can otherwise become established.

Weeding is mostly through a smothering effect when earthing up or spreading compost, but do remove all other weeds as potatoes are growing.

When you feel it is time to harvest, you can remove a few potatoes by feeling around in the soil underneath, from mid-May onwards, leaving the plants to continue growing. Biggest harvests will be from plants that have had time to arrive at the point of maturity, with leaves turning yellow and brown, but blight may force an earlier harvest. Maincrop varieties crop until

TIP: Dry conditions are best for harvesting potatoes to store; otherwise spread them on dry soil or staging, where their skins can dry before you put them in sacks, and then keep them somewhere dry and cool. If there has been blight on leaves, some tubers may be infected and rot later in store, so it is better to eat these quickly.

Green potatoes are mildly poisonous, but a slight greening on one side can be cut off before cooking. When potatoes are stored through a mild winter, some sprouts will grow out of them and need rubbing off before peeling.

September, and are best harvested by the month's end, before slugs cause damage to tubers.

Varieties

First earlies are more about speed than exquisite flavour, but just having fresh potatoes in May and June makes them worthwhile. Also, along with many second earlies, they crop before the arrival of potato blight, so a harvest is assured, although there is some risk of frost damage to leaves in May. Choose the variety that suits your dates and culinary needs.

My favourite is a second early, 'Charlotte', for yield, good taste and keeping quality; I also grow a salad potato such as 'Pink Fir Apple'. The Sarpo varieties are resistant to blight, but their flavour is not remarkable and they have a dry texture.

Possible problems

Blight is a major disease which kills all leaves, probably infecting tubers as well, when there is a week or more of rain and dampness from late June, and in any other wet period until autumn. First signs are some pale brown patches on leaves, which can cover the whole plant within a few days, unless sunshine returns. To prevent blight damage of tubers – brown patches, which quickly spread and cause smelly rotting – it is worth cutting all stems and composting them once you notice the first infection; then harvest tubers on the next dry day.

The harvest in July of one plant of 'Sunrise' potato, a second early variety.

Organic fertilizers

The organic fertilizers listed here have specific uses. They can be a useful addition to compost and manure; many are available as quite expensive proprietary products, and some are possible to find or make yourself.

Blood, fish and bonemeal

This may boost the growth of your plants but is a costly product; I would suggest it is unnecessary if you are spreading compost and manure.

Chicken manure pellets

These are less organic matter and more a concentrated source of nutrients. Use sparingly, perhaps with green waste compost.

Comfrey

You can make your own liquid feed by squashing comfrey leaves into a bucket or barrel, with only a little water, until the liquid turns black. It is often ready to use within a week. Dilute it before watering on to plants in pots; liquid feeds are chiefly for tomatoes and container-grown plants. Stinging nettle

Comfrey provides a natural plant food.

leaves and stems can also be processed in the same way as comfrey to make a rich plant food, but these feeds are extremely smelly and unpleasant to use.

Ericaceous compost

Some plants such as blueberries and cranberries need acid (low pH) soil conditions in order to thrive and crop well. Ericaceous compost is an acidic compost used for growing such plants in enclosed beds or large pots.

Rockdust

Crushed basalt (volcanic rock) has a balanced and wide range of useful minerals; sprinkle it on the surface at any time of year, up to 1cm ($\frac{1}{2}$in) thick if you can afford it. The value of rockdust is hard to quantify; it should give more value on poor soils. Look out for Lavadust, the extremely fine powder of volcanic lava, which I have found is more effective than rockdust.

Seaweed

Coastal residents are well placed for access to one of nature's most complete foods. The rest of us have to make do with occasional use of a proprietary sea product, such as seaweed meal or liquid feed. These products are expensive, but even in small doses the extensive range of minerals they provide can raise plants to a new level of health.

APRIL
week 2

Keeping on top of weeds

The best way to deal with weeds is little and often – frequent, quick weeding, in just a small way, as often as you can. Sorry if this sounds unglamorous and less appealing than planting and picking, but maintaining a productive plot, without undue effort, is really about clever, continual, speedy maintenance, of which a key part is being on top of weed growth at all times. It actually becomes enjoyable when the number of weeds diminishes.

Is this too disciplinarian? Should one not relax more, let nature do its thing and see where it leads? I have seen the results of that approach far too often and know the consequence all too well: a weedy mess where sowing is almost impossible and most of the gardener's time is needed for sorting out the chaos of unwanted plants. Also, in damp climates, there are problems with the slugs that weeds give shelter to.

I have seen gardeners spending huge amounts of time and money on clearing plots, achieving a lovely clean soil, and then demonstrating a seeming aversion to pulling a few weeds, which then drop thousands of seeds. They could have avoided the resulting explosion of weed seedlings by taking only a few minutes to pull their parents.

Hoeing

This is an invaluable skill to develop for the cropping of large plots. When large, almost all weeds are better pulled and removed, but as seedlings they can be hoed. Large weeds are less inclined to die when hoed, as are many grasses, whose roots are amazingly enduring. Since hoeing removes more weeds for less effort, this reinforces the point that weeds are best dealt with small.

HOW TO HOE: Best results come from hoeing when weed roots are young, thin and fragile. The soil needs to be reasonably dry, or the sun bright.

Aim to move as little soil as possible: just enough to disturb or cut through weed roots. If you hoe too deeply, you will simply move weeds, with soil on their roots, to a new location.

Unlike perennial weeds, annuals do not regrow from small roots left in the soil, so the main aim is to cut their stem just below the point where roots branch out in all directions, so that remaining roots become separated and therefore lack any ability to channel growth.

The thin copper blade of an oscillating swivel hoe is easy to push and pull just below the soil surface, to cut weed roots.

Intercropping

It is sometimes possible to sow or plant between rows of a vegetable that has just been sown or planted at a wide spacing, or which is about to finish its growth. This gives you either an extra harvest or an extra month or so in which to achieve a second one, and is simple to manage when soil is clean of weeds. I have enjoyed success with all the following combinations, and there are more to try.

- Parsnips can be sown with a few radish seeds, about one radish every 5cm (2in): the radishes grow and mature before parsnip seedlings are of medium size. Also the fast-emerging radishes help to identify the row(s) of parsnip seeds before they come up.
- Lettuce can be planted in late spring at the same time as, and between, kale or Brussels sprouts, which allows enough time for lettuce hearts to grow or leaves to be picked before the brassicas cover them over.
- Sweetcorn can be planted (this is better than sowing) in the gaps between winter squash. Plant both at the same time: two sweetcorn for each squash plant, set 1m (39in) apart.
- Carrots and beetroot can be sown between rows of maturing garlic in early June, by which time the garlic leaves will be starting to go yellow. Seedlings should be showing true leaves by the time you harvest the garlic bulbs. A variation on this is to plant parsley, beetroot, dwarf beans

Planting dill in gaps between radish seedlings in early April.

or swedes between the garlic in early to mid-June.
- Garlic can be grown with parsley under cover in winter: plant parsley in September at its usual spacing of 25–30cm (10–12in) and then plant garlic cloves between the small parsley plants in October. They will all survive winter together and you can pick parsley from February to May, then pull it out when rising to flower, leaving the garlic to mature in early July.
- I have also managed to grow lettuce under cucumbers: the lettuces are smaller than usual but of good quality.

How to grow:
LETTUCE

Lettuce in 3cm (1in) modules ready to plant. Left to right: 'Grenoble Red', 'Chartwell', 'Rosemoor', 'Red Sails' and 'Freckles'.

WHERE & WHEN TO SOW: Sow direct from March, or indoors February–July.

TIME FROM SOWING TO PLANTING: 4–6 weeks.

WHEN TO PLANT & SPACING: April–August; 22–30cm (9–12in) when growing for hearts; 20–22cm (8–9in) when growing for leaves. Lettuce seed is small and light and grows best when left uncovered. Lettuce can be sown as early as February indoors and from about mid-March outdoors. Indoor sowings can be in a tray or pots of moist compost, and then covered with glass or a polythene bag for up to a week, by which time roots will be developing and first leaves visible. Speed of growth is closely related to freshness of seed.

CARE: Outdoor sowings need covering with soil, but only a little, and watering every five days or so in dry weather. After 4–6 weeks, plants can be thinned when they are still small but perhaps large enough to eat.

TIP: Lettuce seed can become dormant when sown in hot weather. Water the drill before sowing and sow in mid- to late afternoon during very hot spells.

Lettuce for hearts

The only difference between growing lettuce for hearts rather than leaves is a slightly wider spacing and an earlier last sowing date, as lettuce for hearts should not normally be sown after early August.

For a few hearts at all times, sow monthly from March to June and then fortnightly in July. Sow a few seeds of different varieties, because they will mature at slightly different times. Aim to cut hearts before they turn too pale and dense, as some leaves are prone to rot at that stage: browning at the edges of heart leaves (known as tipburn) is often caused by a shortage of moisture, so give extra water as hearts swell.

Lettuce for leaves

The number of varieties available means a wide choice of flavour and colour: 'Bijou' and 'Rosemoor' for dark red leaves, 'Freckles' and 'Mottistone' for speckled colour – and the leaves of 'Freckles' are sweet, as are those of many green cos varieties such as 'Chartwell'. It is worth browsing through a catalogue or on the internet, bearing in mind that all varieties offered as hearting lettuce can also be picked for leaves. For a harvest of winter leaves indoors, sow seeds in early September.

How to grow:
CARROTS

A carrot harvest of (left to right) 'Maestro', 'Honeysnax', 'Purple Haze' and 'Nantes'.

WHERE & WHEN TO SOW: Sow carrots direct where they are to mature. For early carrots, sow late March–April. For winter roots, sow ideally in mid-June.

SPACING: For early carrots, 2–3 seeds per 1cm (¹/₂in) in rows of 30cm (12in). Thin after a month to one seedling per 1cm (¹/₂in). For winter roots, sow two seeds per 1cm (¹/₂in) in rows of 25–30cm (10–12in), thin after a month to one seedling per 1cm (¹/₂in); leave more space if you want really large carrots.

CARE: Small carrot seeds are slow to grow and are often appreciated by slugs; if you come through that test, the carrot root fly awaits; if your carrots avoid them, you will enjoy a treat, because freshly pulled carrots are superior to anything you can buy.

Having clean soil pays off when sowing carrots because the tiny seedlings are so easily smothered by weed growth. If the soil is full of weed seeds, wait for some to germinate in April, and then hoe them off, two or three times at fortnightly intervals if there are masses; then sow carrots in June for winter use.

Early April is often a good time for first sowings, when the soil has warmed a little and slugs are therefore less likely to eat seedlings. Tiny, thin leaves should be visible within ten days, but stay small for a month. If they don't appear, slugs have probably eaten them and resowing is required.

With summer sowings you may need to water in the bottom of drills before sowing the seed; otherwise be measly with the water to encourage sweetness.

Weeding is vital for carrot seedlings and, even when carrots are growing strongly, keep pulling any weeds you see to prevent them seeding.

Harvest carrots from the third week in June until November.

Potting on tender plants

Most vegetables can be planted out in their permanent positions at the size they reach in modules, plugs and small pots, but a few vegetables are best potted on and kept in the propagating area until they are much larger. This mainly applies to vegetables that need extra warmth, such as tomato and pepper plants.

To pot on a plant, three-quarters fill a slightly but not significantly larger pot with compost and make a suitable-sized hole to receive the plant you are moving on. Tap or push out the root ball of the plant you want to pot on from below, keeping the soil ball round the roots intact as far as possible. Gently place it in the pre-made hole in the new pot and firm it in. Bury any long stems in the new compost to make the plants sturdier, as roots will spring from the buried stem.

Spread out the new pots to allow them to receive light from all sides. Then after two or three weeks, if it is still too early for final planting, you can move the plants again into slightly larger pots.

> **TIP:** I have often noticed that it works better to repot twice, each time into a slightly larger pot, than to repot once into a much larger pot, probably because it is easier to avoid overwatering in smaller pots. Perhaps plants also appreciate the extra attention and handling.

Potting on: a small tomato plant grown in a 2.5cm (1in) module being put into a 5cm (2in) module.

Creating
no-dig beds

You can purchase kits of bed sides, but they are expensive, and I recommend making your own where possible. It's not difficult, as I explain here. As long as water can drain away, beds may be sited anywhere that is reasonably level. Placing them on grass, gravel or even on paving stones without concrete grout are all fine, but soil underneath, which may initially be undug lawn or weeds, gives best results.

On sloping ground, I find it best to orientate beds down the slope and not across it. This makes watering and compost spreading easier, with less tendency for added materials to spill over the lower edges. On flat ground, as long as access to paths is not impeded, orient beds north–south so that sunlight is shared between all crops of different heights.

Edges

If you are making beds with sides, the most viable and natural material is wood. I recommend that you purchase untreated wooden planks, or scavenge old ones, and then paint on a plant-safe wood finishing product that is free of synthetic chemicals.

Wooden sides can be 2.5–5cm (1–2in) thick. Thicker is better for durability and for straightness of long edges, but I caution against using sleepers: their extra thickness makes it harder to reach the middle of beds, and they also mostly contain creosote, which may seep out.

The bed sides are best 15cm (6in) deep for all vegetables. Most people find widths of 1–1.2m (3–4ft) work well for access from both sides.

Plastic is sometimes used as edging. Its advantage over wood is that it allows better retention of moisture; this can also prevent overheating of dry bed sides in the summer. But there is some uncertainty over how long it endures without flexing or becoming brittle.

I do not recommend bricks and stones, because they are heavier to handle and harbour too many slugs.

Contents

After the expense and trouble of assembling a bed, it is worth putting something richer than soil inside it. I would avoid using more than 50 per cent 'topsoil' of unknown quality. Do use any spare soil of your own, freshly removed and put straight into the bed. Generally I find that animal manure and compost give more vigorous and generally healthier plants, except for pure green waste, which has too few nutrients.

Organic matter should be reasonably well rotted, with lumpy ingredients at the bottom and finer compost spread as a top layer of 2.5–5cm (1–2in). I do not prescribe exact ingredients, because all these ingredients are heavy and expensive to transport, and what you use will depend on what is available locally. To fill several beds, you need to buy in bulk rather than in sacks: a bed of

1.25 x 2.5m (4 x 8ft) contains a good half ton of ingredients, depending on wetness.

Filling beds

The contents of a 15cm (6in) deep bed will be sufficient to smother the attempted regrowth of grass and weeds – though you may need to trowel out regrowth of perennial weeds at first.

All the contents should be firmed down, so that plants have a roothold and the bed retains moisture and holds an increased quantity of ingredients. Walking on a bed's contents is the best way to firm them and would hurt only if they were saturated with water. If the ingredients are wet, I walk on a plank to press them down, in order to spread my weight.

A good final profile is slightly domed upwards, the middle about 10cm (4in) higher than the edges, because, even after being well trodden, the contents will be settling downwards for months afterwards.

Subsequent maintenance

With a bed filled this way, no digging or cultivation of any kind is necessary. It should be easy to keep weeds almost to zero, by pulling out any little ones as soon as they are visible, and they will slide easily out of the soft surface.

After a year of cropping it will take another 2.5–5cm (1–2in) of compost to keep the bed as full as it was. You need to repeat this every year, either in autumn, or whenever there is clear space.

MAKING A NO-DIG RAISED BED

1 In December, the wooden boards were placed on grass and filled with compost.

2 When using compost and manure, 'overfill' the beds, then press down.

3 Using a manure fork to break lumps after frost has thawed.

4 By May the bed is producing salad onions, lettuce, pea shoots and spinach.

APRIL
week 4

APRIL
Jobs for the month

Be prepared for both winter and summer in April: even if it is cold there is still much to do, especially removing or mulching any new growth of perennial weeds, first plantings with fleece on top and new sowings under cover.

CLEARING: Remove leek trimmings, winter cabbage and Brussels sprout stalks, and flowering winter salad plants.

WEEDING: General hoeing of weed seedlings is possible whenever soil is reasonably dry; continue removing perennial weeds.

COMPOSTING: Assuming the rest of your plot is already composted, new compost is needed only where ground has just been cleared: for example, after harvesting leeks and Brussels sprouts.

RAKING/FORKING: As for January unless you have a reasonably fine tilth already.

SOWING: Similar to March indoors, adding courgettes, squash, cucumber, basil around mid-month; also leeks, carrots and beetroot outdoors. But avoid sowing all your seed – wait until May and June to sow summer beans and winter brassicas.

PLANTING: Potatoes of all kinds, calabrese, cauliflower, beetroot, globe artichoke, peas, beetroot, lettuce, broad beans, onions, spinach.

WATERING: Under cloches of overwintered salads.

HARVESTING: The final leeks, savoy cabbages and purple sprouting; asparagus by month's end; plenty of salad leaves indoors, but plants may also be flowering and many finish cropping by late April.

Salad plants in April in an unheated polytunnel. They have been regularly harvested since November.

MAY

MAY is a hungry month with
winter vegetables finished
and spring sowings barely
ready. Welcome exceptions are
overwintered cabbage, spinach
and onions, and first plantings
of spinach, lettuce and peas
for shoots. After the middle
of the month you can sow
French beans, sweetcorn and
courgettes. Perennial vegetables
come into their own, including
kales and asparagus.

How to grow: BASIL

WHERE & WHEN TO SOW: Sow indoors April–June.

TIME FROM SOWING TO PLANTING: 5–7 weeks.

WHEN TO PLANT & SPACING: Late May–July in shelter; 20–30cm (8–12in).

CARE: Basil needs heat at all stages, and dry air to grow healthily. So it is never worth sowing outdoors in spring, and even in a greenhouse I wait until the middle of April.

Seed can be sown in a tray and pricked out: keep seedlings and small plants growing in gentle warmth and be careful to water sparingly. There is no rush to plant basil outside until summer is well under way, so plants usually need potting on before planting. Handle carefully because they have fragile roots.

Basil grows best in full sun, under cover if possible, either direct in the soil in a greenhouse, or in containers.

There is a huge choice of varieties, with a wide range of different flavours,

TIP: Tall, cordon tomatoes can be underplanted with small bush or Greek basil, which, although never able to grow abundantly in the tomatoes' shade, offers tasty leaves and probably helps the tomato plants to grow more healthily.

leaf sizes and shapes. You can choose from flavours of cinnamon, lemon, spice, lime and liquorice; the large lettuce-leaved basil or tiny-leaved Greek or bush basil; the serrated, crinkly leaved 'Green Ruffles' or its striking coloured counterpart 'Purple Ruffles' . . . there is seemingly an endless choice! The long-established sweet or Genovese basil is still one of the most productive.

To keep plants young and productive, pick leaves and stems regularly. Flowering shoots need to be removed as soon as they become apparent.

Sweet basil in 2.5cm (1in) modules, ready to pot on.

Time to plant out

The ultimate act of propagating plants from seed indoors is setting plants in their final destination, where they are to grow and crop. This process has three stages: hardening off, planting and transition.

Hardening off

This entails setting trays and pots of plants that have been raised under cover in a slightly sheltered place outside, whatever the weather, for two or three days before they are planted in their final positions in the open. Such hardening off allows the plants to acclimatize gradually to the cooler temperatures outdoors and helps to prevent a sudden shock at the change of growing conditions that may slow down a plant's growth severely or even kill the plant.

No hardening off is needed when planting outdoors and covering at once with fleece or a cloche. I have taken courgettes out of my greenhouse and planted them in cold soil, laid fleece on top and they grew fine.

Planting

Planting involves making holes in the soil with a dibber for modules and plugs, or with a trowel for larger root balls, and pushing plants in firmly. All pot- and module-grown plants benefit from being planted a little below surface level. For plants with long stems, such as brassicas and tomatoes, make the holes deep enough so that you can bury the stem well. This helps to anchor plants in place and will make them stronger.

Transition

For about a week after planting, plants look a little fragile and growth is scarcely visible, although new roots are forming undergound. Then suddenly a healthy lustre reappears in the leaves and from then on new growth is rapid.

Module-grown plants ready to plant, of mizuna, red mustard and pak choi.

How to grow: PEAS

WHERE & WHEN TO SOW: Sow indoors March–early May, or sow direct April–May, either in dibbed holes 2.5cm (1in) deep or a drill of that depth.

TIME FROM SOWING TO PLANTING: 3 weeks.

WHEN TO PLANT & SPACING: April–May, 10–15 x 60–150cm (4–6 x 24–60in).

CARE: Make March sowings indoors in modules or small pots; after planting out, these thrive under a fleece cover, which can also be used over direct outdoor sowings. Mice and birds love pea seed, so it is worth having a mousetrap nearby when sowing indoors. I sow two or three seeds per module and transplant without thinning at the spacings above: the wider spacing is for tall varieties of pea, growing to a height of 2m (7ft).

Alternatively sow seed outdoors from April to mid-May, covering seeds and plants with fleece until they need support. Later sowing is possible, but quality and yield will be lower.

Soil can be enriched with extra organic matter on top, because peas love compost mulches for their ability to hold extra moisture. Water is often needed, especially for tall varieties, which consume large amounts.

Support is needed according to the size of the variety grown. This can be provided by hazel branches or poles, or netting; peas can also be grown up wigwams, spaced as for climbing beans, but with some string meshed around the sticks in a cobweb fashion, for tendrils to hang on to.

Always check a variety's height, to be sure of having the ones you want. Round-seeded varieties such as 'Feltham First' are early to crop, but with less sweetness than wrinkle-seeded varieties such as 'Greenshaft' (bush), 'Alderman' (tall), 'Mr Bray' (tall heritage) and 'Tall Sugar Snap'.

TIP: Early sowings often do best because they tend to avoid the peak times for both pea moth and mildew, which can spoil crops, though usually neither problem is catastrophic.

Tall yellow and purple peas growing up tripods of hazel poles.

MAY
week 1

Salads:
PLANNING CROPS

Salad plants grow quickly and offer many meals for less effort and in less space than many other vegetables. Within each season you can have a wide range of salad leaves, all with wonderfully different flavours – flavours of home-grown leaves are richer and stronger than those of bought salads.

SALAD LEAVES (sown and grown outdoors)					
Salad (* = oriental leaves)	Family (see page 168)	Best sow	Harvest outdoor	Qualities	Tips
Basil	Mint	Apr–May in, Jun out	Jul–Sep	Big flavours, many choices	Keep plants warm and dry
Chard/leaf beet/beetroot	Beet	Apr–Aug	May–Oct, Mar–Apr	Colours better than flavour	Pick small
Chicory, forcing	Lettuce	May–Jun	Nov–Dec, Jan–Apr	Yellow, crunchy	Force in darkness
Chicory, heart	Lettuce	Jun–25 Jul	Aug–Nov	Stores well	Fertile soil
Chicory, leaf	Lettuce	Jun–Aug	Jul–Apr	Winter hardy	Pick small
Chinese cabbage, heart*	Brassica	Jul	Sep–Nov	Crisp leaf, dense heart	Cover against insects
Coriander & chervil	Umbellifer	Jul–Aug	Sep–Apr	Winter hardy	'Calypso' coriander for a long harvest
Dill	Umbellifer	Mar–May	May–Jul	Early, fragrant	Sow in spring
Endive, heart	Lettuce	Jun–Jul	Sep–Nov	Large plants	Sow in summer
Endive, leaf	Lettuce	Jun–Aug	Jul–Apr	Disease free	Pick small
Kale, flat leaf	Brassica	Jun–Jul	Sep–May	Winter hardy	Spring flowers
Komatsuna*	Brassica	Aug	Sep–Nov	Fast, tender	Slug prone
Lamb's lettuce/corn salad	Valerian	Aug	Oct–Apr	Hardiest salad plant	Sow direct in late August

SALAD LEAVES (sown and grown outdoors)					
Salad (* = oriental leaves)	Family (see page 168)	Best sow	Harvest outdoor	Qualities	Tips
Land cress	Brassica	Jul–Aug	Sep–Apr	Strong taste	Pigeon cover
Lettuce, heart	Lettuce	Mar–Jul	Jun–Oct	Sweet heart	Frequent sowing
Lettuce, leaf	Lettuce	Mar–Aug	May–Oct	Many harvests at 22cm (9in)	Pick outer leaves, no knife
Mizuna & mibuna*	Brassica	Aug	Sep–Nov, Apr	Hardy, tasty	Many varieties
Mustard*	Brassica	Aug	Sep–Nov, Apr	Pungent flavour	Pick small, many colours
Onion, salad	Allium	Mar–Jun, end Aug	May–Sep, Apr–May	Long harvest, hardy plants	Sow early or late
Orach	Beet	Feb–Apr	Apr–Jul	Vibrant colour	Avoid seeding
Pak choi & tatsoi*	Brassica	Jul–Aug	Aug–Nov	Varietal choices	Cover against insects
Parsley	Umbellifer	Mar–Jul	Jun–May	Long season	Flat or curled
Peas, for shoots	Legume	Mar–Jun	May–Aug	Rich pea flavour	Sow early for most shoots
Purslane, summer	Moss rose	Jun–Jul	Jul–Sep	Succulent	Needs dry weather
Purslane, winter	Claytonia	Aug	Oct–Apr	Hardy, tender	Cover from October
Radish, leaf*	Brassica	Aug–Sep	Sep–Nov	Abundant	Roots edible
Rocket, salad	Brassica	Aug	Sep–Apr	Hot flavour	Sow in Aug for healthy leaf
Rocket, wild	Brassica	Jul	Sep–Jun	Spring harvests	Wider spacing
Sorrel	Oxalis	Mar–Jul	Feb–Nov	Lemon taste	Buckler-leaved is good for salads
Spinach	Beet	Mar–Apr, Jul	Apr–Jun, Sep–May	Winter hardy	Remove slugs
Tree spinach	Beet	Mar–Apr	May–Sep	Colourful shoots	Pick shoots frequently

How to grow: SWEETCORN

WHERE & WHEN TO SOW: Sow indoors mid-April–May, or sow direct May–early June.

TIME FROM SOWING TO PLANTING: 2–3 weeks.

WHEN TO PLANT & SPACING: May–July, 30–38cm (12–15in). An even spacing of plants, for example in four rows along a 1.2m (4ft) bed, allows pollen to fall from flowers in summer and to drop evenly on the cobs' tassels, making for a full complement of kernels.

CARE: Sweetcorn needs warmth. In much of Britain this means sowing outdoors in late May or early June, which gives only just enough time for cobs to mature, except in a hot summer. Reliable harvests come from sowing indoors after mid-April, to plant out from early May, and a fleece cover will help these plantings until early June, unless it is unusually warm.

The soil needs to be moisture-retentive and with a mulch of compost on top.

Watering is beneficial if the soil is really dry in August and early September.

Support is not necessary for the strong, woody stems. Weeding is needed around and under sweetcorn with some hoeing and hand weeding, even in summer when the plants are tall and vigorous, to prevent any seeding.

There are few pests of sweetcorn, although slugs sometimes eat early sowings. As cobs ripen, badgers and birds become interested – hopefully only birds because there is no remedy for badgers except a minimum 1.2m (4ft) wall or sturdy fence.

Cropping will be from August for early varieties in a warm summer, until October for later varieties and in cool summers. When the cobs' tassels are turning dark brown, the kernels will be mature and should be both sweet and full. If you pick earlier the kernels will be smaller and of a paler colour; if you pick later the kernels will be dark yellow with less sugar and more starch – mealies.

A cob of sweetcorn 'Sweet Nugget' F1. There is a good combination here of tender sweetness and full-bodied kernels

TIP: Sweetcorn plants, raised in small pots, can be planted between trailing squashes in late May and early June.

How to grow:
DWARF FRENCH BEANS

WHERE & WHEN TO SOW: Sow indoors early May, for earliest harvests, or the second half of May for more reliable crops. Outdoor sowings are most successful from early June. A last sowing in late June should provide plenty of beans in September and even October if mild.

TIME FROM SOWING TO PLANTING: 2–3 weeks.

WHEN TO PLANT & SPACING: Plant early May sowings after mid-May; later May sowings in early June. A June planting from an indoor sowing in the second half of May often works better, because these plants thrive in warm soil and are knocked back by any cold nights below 6–8°C (43–46°F). Space at 30–38cm (12–15in).

CARE: Sow in trays of large modules or in small pots. You can set plants out when still small, 5–7cm (2–3in) high, rather than potting on to make large plants. The first planting of dwarf beans in mid-May can be covered with fleece for 2–3 weeks, to speed up establishment and bring the harvest forward a week or two.

Add plenty of organic matter to the soil to help hold moisture and water plants thoroughly in dry spells. Warm weather is vital for these plants to crop well. The bushy plants do not normally need support, but sometimes some twiggy sticks are useful to keep larger plants upright; this also helps to keep the lowest beans off the soil where they might rot or be attacked by slugs. Remove weeds as you see them.

Pick the beans when young and slender; allowing them to remain on the plant too long will make them stringier and coarser. Frequent picking helps to keep the plants cropping longer.

TIP: Dwarf beans are a good vegetable for medium to large containers, but watch for slugs nibbling them hard in wet summers.

French beans ready to plant out. I sowed two seeds per module and thinned to the strongest.

MAY
week 3

A year of harvests from two undug beds

In 2012 my experimental beds entered their sixth season, and this is a description of how the two undug beds fared. After a fine and warm March, good for the first sowings and plantings, it was an endlessly wet year apart from one lovely spell in late May: slugs were prevalent from April and growth diminished 10 per cent from 2011 levels, because of low temperatures and lack of sunshine.

Plant health was good as organic matter had built up over five years; both drainage and moisture retention were increased by extra carbon in the soil. A soil test in late 2010 showed organic matter of 6.8 per cent in the undug beds, compared with 4.8 per cent when I began.

Parsnips harvested from the experimental beds in November: dug bed in front and undug behind.

The column totals show a spread of harvests throughout the year, and kale would have gone on, but I needed to dig the adjacent dug beds. This highlights another advantage of no dig – that soil preparation can be done while winter greens are still cropping. I spread compost around kale, leeks and Brussels sprouts in late autumn, so that after their last harvest in spring the soil/compost surface was soft and crumbly, ready for plantings.

The monthly columns also hide the storage potential of vegetables like onion, celeriac and parsnip, which keep for many months, so a third of these beds' output was food for winter.

The figures for salad are good, from a small area. The lettuce consisted of just eighteen plants of 'Freckles', 'Chartwell' and 'Bergamo', picked weekly of their outer leaves, and they cropped for longer than usual thanks to the wet summer. All of the first plantings and sowings were made by the third week in March and beds were then covered with fleece for one month. I weeded carefully after removing the fleece and was nervous for a while about how plants would fare in the cold rain of late April and early May, but they were well enough established to weather that period and then grow strongly after mid-May.

Comparison with the two dug beds in 2012

Total harvests from the same vegetables growing alongside in the two dug beds were 61.75kg (136lb), compared with 67.01kg (148lb) from the two undug beds of the same size. Main differences were from extra slug damage in the dug beds to, for example, the carrots sown in March. Most autumn salads were also badly affected on the dug soil, but the spring lettuce gave slightly more leaves from dug soil, and so did parsnips; everything else was a little less.

Altogether it was an excellent year for well-fed, undug soil and showed how resilient this method is, because results are good in dry years too!

MONTHLY HARVESTS FROM ONE 1.5 X 2.5M (5 X 8FT) UNDUG BED									
Vegetable	Apr	May	Jun	Jul	Aug	Sep	Oct	Nov	Total kg
Carrot, early				1.15					1.15
French bean*						1.05	0.14		1.19
Lettuce	1.60	3.13	4.25	2.68	0.40				12.06
Kale*							1.65	1.26	2.91
Parsnip								10.95	10.95
Potato, early			4.67						4.67
Radish	0.62								0.62
Spinach	0.21	1.38	1.28						2.87
TOTALS kg (equals 2.2lb)	2.43	4.51	10.20	3.83	0.40	1.05	1.79	12.21	36.42

* Succession crop.

MONTHLY HARVESTS FROM A SECOND 1.5 X 2.5M (5 X 8FT) UNDUG BED									
Vegetable	Apr	May	Jun	Jul	Aug	Sep	Oct	Nov	Total kg
Beetroot			1.60	2.12					3.72
Cabbage, early*		1.86							1.86
Cabbage, winter								1.26	1.26
Celeriac							4.60		4.60
Chervil*						0.18	0.26	0.09	0.53
Endive*					0.77	1.59	0.62		2.98
Onion				7.25					7.25
Pea 'Tall Sugar Pea'			1.97	5.75					7.72
Wild rocket*						0.12	0.55		0.67
TOTALS kg (equals 2.2lb)		1.86	3.57	15.12	0.77	1.89	6.03	1.35	30.59

Some common annual weeds

This selection is to help you identify and deal with some likely and unwanted appearances in your plot. Ideally you will hoe them when they are very small, and after a year of doing that your soil will have far fewer weed seedlings.

Bittercress

Hairy bittercress

(*Cardamine hirsuta*)
DESCRIPTION: 2.5–5cm (1–2in) high, tiny, white flowers.
SEEDING: Sets seed in 4–6 weeks.

Mostly a winter weed of cool, moist soil, small enough to go unnoticed until it scatters hundreds of long-lived seeds at a young age, so keep an eye out for it in spells of consistently damp and cool weather. The small leaves are edible and tasty.

Charlock

(*Brassica arvensis*)
DESCRIPTION: To 60cm (24in) high, pale yellow flowers.
SEEDING: Sets seed in 8–10 weeks.

Germinates all through the seasons, mostly in spring, and can also overwinter. A fast-growing weed of the brassica family, often full of flea beetle damage but still able to set hundreds of seeds. Easy to hoe when small and easy to pull when larger, but don't underestimate its ability to gain ground through numerical superiority.

Charlock

Chickweed

(*Stellaria media*)
DESCRIPTION: 5–7cm (2–3in) high, vigorous spreading habit, small, white flowers, strong root system.
SEEDING: Can set seed within a month.

Probably the most common annual weed, chickweed germinates in damp soil, chiefly in early spring and autumn and in mild winters too. The odd plant here and there is easy to remove but its ability to set seed quickly can lead to problems, because it is often too damp for hoeing when chickweed grows. Watch for it at all times and hoe seedlings or pull any small plants you see, with a firm tug because they have tenacious, if shallow roots.

Chickweed

Annual meadow grass

(*Poa annua*)
DESCRIPTION: 2.5–5cm (1–2in) high, tiny feathery flowers.
SEEDING: Sets seed in 6–8 weeks in any season.

A small, tough and common plant, growing whenever it is mild and moist for a couple of weeks. Roots are numerous but superficial, survive waterlogging but dislike drought. Common in mild winters and in any other damp season, annual meadow grass is difficult to hoe and is best pulled when small. Larger clumps have tenacious roots, which hang on to a lot of soil – a bad loss to the garden and a bad addition to the compost heap, where any larger amounts of soil can slow heating and decomposition of the other ingredients.

Annual meadow grass

Groundsel

(*Senecio vulgaris*)
DESCRIPTION: 5–22cm (2–9in) high, clustered, small, yellow flowers.
SEEDING: Sets seed within 4–6 weeks.

An easy weed to hoe but not to be underestimated, because even one plant, setting hundreds of seeds after only a few weeks' growth, can lead to much extra weeding in subsequent years. Germinates at all times except midwinter, mostly in fertile soil; sets seed when small and young if soil is dry or shady. Check for odd plants under leaves of, for example, parsnips, courgettes and asparagus. Go hunt them! Remove any with flowers, because they can still make viable seed if uprooted but left on the soil.

Groundsel

Common field speedwell

(*Veronica persica*)
DESCRIPTION: Ground-hugging spring and autumn weed, slender stems, pale blue flowers.
SEEDING: Sets seed in 4–6 weeks.

Of the many kinds of speedwell, including perennial ones, this common annual is the most likely to grow, in early spring and late autumn, and is not too difficult to hoe or pull out when small, mostly from March to May, but becomes difficult if allowed to establish as larger clumps of many plants. Slender speedwell looks similar but does not set seed and spreads by root fragments.

Common field speedwell

MAY
Jobs for the month

May is when growth takes off, but you never know in advance when that will be, and it is easy to fall behind when there is sudden warmth. Be prepared with plants, keep soil clean and you will be fine.

CLEARING: Remove last overwintered kale, purple sprouting broccoli, chard, spinach and overwintered salads.

WEEDING: Many weeds grow fast in May, so you will find yourself hoeing, hand weeding and also cutting or pulling grass along plot edges; be vigilant about weeds from now on, as their speed of growth in warmer weather can easily result in a plot being 'taken over' and you then become discouraged, whereas dealing with them when small is easier and encourages good morale.

COMPOSTING: Do this after any clearing, where the soil has no compost residue on the surface, and to 'earth up' potatoes.

SOWING INDOORS OR OUTDOORS Brussels sprouts, autumn cabbage and sweetcorn; then wait until mid-month to sow runner and French beans and cucumber indoors, or early June outdoors.

PLANTING: Indoor plants such as tomatoes and aubergines can be planted; courgettes, squashes, celery and celeriac can be planted outdoors as long as all risk of frost has passed.

STAKING: Stake early peas and broad beans in windy areas, when 30cm (1ft) and 60cm (2ft) high respectively.

WATERING: Mainly for plants newly set out and for salad plants.

HARVESTING: Salad leaves, spinach, radish, asparagus, rhubarb, overwintered cabbage and salad onion; now is the time known as the 'hungry gap'.

Squash plants were covered with fleece for eighteen days in May but only a few small weeds grew and I am pulling them all.

JUNE

JUNE starts an exciting period
as plants grow strongly and
offer the first, tasty harvests
of small carrots, beetroot, peas
and broad beans and also late
in the month the main harvest
of garlic. Find time for extra
weeding if weeds threaten to
get ahead of you, keeping soil
clean at all times. Apart from
pea shoots and courgettes for
summer crops, sow carrots,
beetroot and swede for
eating in winter.

Harvesting
salad crops

You can allow salad leaves to grow as large as you like them. Thickly sown seedlings can be cut at the two-leaf stage – stems and all. Called micro leaves, these are expensive and time-consuming to produce, because harvests are small, with a need for frequent resowing, using plenty of seeds.

How to pick leaves

Careful picking makes as much or more difference to the size and quality of harvest as does the effort put into growing plants in the first place. There are two options: cutting, or picking outer leaves.

CUTTING: If you allow plants to grow thickly in 25cm (10in) rows, say 2.5cm (1in) apart, the maximum harvest will probably be two or three cuts of all leaves, and you will need to grade out some of the yellowing lower leaves. Gather a handful of leaves and slice a knife horizontally just underneath your fingers, always cutting just above the smallest leaves you can see, not into the stem, so that regrowth is possible. Salads that regrow most quickly and healthily after cutting are chicory, endive, mizuna, mibuna, rocket, sorrel and winter purslane. Cutting is a useful way of tidying up an overgrown plant: first, cut out the healthy leaves; then you can cut and remove all older and yellowing leaves to allow a clean start, for easier picking next time.

PICKING OUTER LEAVES:
1. Plant at a 22cm (9in) spacing.
2. Leave to grow until the plants' outer leaves are touching or nearly touching.
3. Gently twist or pinch off all larger leaves. On this first pick, a few of the outermost leaves are often somewhat damaged by slugs or disease – a one-off problem of the first pick: remove these leaves and compost.
4. Then after a week or so you can again pick the newly grown outer and larger leaves in this same way. The central, younger, smaller leaves keep growing into new harvests, every week during the growing season and for 2–3 months, with leaves in good health.

How to pick hearts

Large, hearting plants need extra moisture, and are more prone to diseases that cause rotting of some heart leaves, so it is worth cutting the first hearts of each sowing of lettuce, endive and chicory before they are fully firm. This gives a week or more of harvests before plants are fully mature and decreases the risk of some hearts spoiling or flowering before you can eat them.

Frequency of picking

In warm, bright weather growth is rapid and new leaves may be picked every 5–7 days, compared with every 2–4 weeks in winter, when precious new growth is much helped by you picking rather than cutting leaves.

In winter some salad plants such as mustards, rocket and mizuna grow noticeably more quickly than others such as lamb's lettuce, chard and salad onion.

How to keep leaves fresh after harvest

Leaves are still alive after being picked and continue living for many days in cool dampness. To store them for later use, mix and wash in a container of cold water, drain the water out in a colander or spin it out, bag up any leaves that are not needed immediately and keep the bag in a fridge, or a cool but unfrozen outdoor space in winter. At temperatures of 2–10°C (36–50°F) bagged leaves will stay alive for up to a week, especially when they have been grown in healthy soil.

TIP: After cutting a heart out of lettuce, endive and chicory, more leaves appear from stems left in the soil. With endives in late summer, it is possible to cut almost-mature hearts just above the smallest leaves, gathering all leaves except the tiniest heart ones, and then have subsequent regrowth, even to hearting stage again.

LETTUCE FROM SOWING TO HARVEST

1 A selection of module-raised lettuce being planted in mid-June.

2 Three weeks later the lettuces are ready for a first pick.

3 The first pick: the outer leaves have been twisted off and any weeds removed.

4 Five weeks later, after several more picks, the lettuce are still growing.

How to grow:
RUNNER & CLIMBING FRENCH BEANS

WHERE & WHEN TO SOW: Sow indoors May or sow direct June–early July.

TIME FROM SOWING TO PLANTING: 2–3 weeks.

WHEN TO PLANT & SPACING: June–July; 30cm (12in) in double rows or wigwams with space around to pick.

CARE: Climbing beans are sensitive to temperature and wind, so, if your plot is exposed, dwarf French beans are a better choice. All runner and French bean plants are killed by frost and do not grow in cold soil, hence my advice to be patient with sowing, even if it suddenly warms up in early May: wait until mid-month because there is nearly always some cold weather until the end of May, even in the south-east of Britain.

Runner bean 'Stenner' in August. The flowers suggest there are more beans to come.

Sow seeds individually in small pots from mid-May, under cover for extra warmth to help germination, or from June outside. Soil for growing can be just like every other vegetable, with a surface mulch of compost. It is often advised to make a trench and fill it with organic matter, which works but is not necessary unless you have dry soil. You can put supports in place beforehand or once plants are growing.

Once established plants send up leaders and may need help to find the poles – gently twist the running stems around a little. Then growth is fast and flowering in July is pretty, soon followed by repeat harvests at whatever size you like the pods. Pick twice a week in hot weather and give some water to prolong harvests. Search hard for bean pods, which often hide behind leaves.

In hot summers, July sowings are good for beans in early autumn when the flowers set more reliably, because runner bean flowers in particular often drop off when nights are too warm, or when soil is too dry.

TIP: If you don't pick pods of Borlotti French bean, Czar runner bean and some other varieties, their pods will fill and then dry on the plant. You can harvest them in October for dry beans in winter.

JUNE
week 1

JUNE
week 2

How to grow:
PEAS FOR SHOOTS

WHERE & WHEN TO SOW: Sow indoors February–June or sow direct March–June.

TIME FROM SOWING TO PLANTING: 2–4 weeks.

WHEN TO PLANT & SPACING: March–July; 20–30cm (8–12in).

CARE: Once you master the knack of picking them, pea shoots become an easy and delicious addition to salads, and when you grow an abundance they are delicious lightly steamed, for an early taste of pea, long before any peas are even developing.

Sow tall varieties only, to have a longer season of decent length shoots. My favourite is 'Tall Sugar Pea', and other good varieties are 'Alderman' and 'Mr Bray' if you can find some seed. Seeds maintain their viability for many years and can be saved (see page 138). This is worthwhile because I have suffered problems of poor germination with bought pea seeds, whereas my own just leap out of the ground.

First sowings can be under cover and a windowsill is ideal for giving them enough warmth to germinate, as early as January in milder areas, for growing indoors; sowings in January can be planted in a greenhouse or polytunnel in February, for shoots by early April.

Sow two or three seeds in each module or small pot, harden plants off when 5cm (2in) high by leaving them outside for 3–4 days, and then plant out as clumps and cover with fleece. Peas survive frost and snow, but fleece helps them to establish more quickly and provides protection from pigeons too.

When plants are 15–25cm (6–10in) high, harvest the top 5cm (2in) of stem. Then be patient while plants recover. By May you can be picking a few pea shoots each week, followed by abundance in June, until the shoots become thin and sinewy in July as plants try to make seed instead. Harvests of actual peas are small when you have been picking pea shoots.

Peas for shoots being planted between lettuces 'Fristina' (left) and 'Mottistone' (right).

TIP: Spring sowings are the most productive. Sowings in June and July make smaller amounts of leaf and shoot before they want to flower and they are also at risk of mildew on leaves.

How to grow:
CHARD & BEETROOT

WHERE & WHEN TO SOW: Sow direct or indoors late April–July.

TIME FROM SOWING TO PLANTING: 3–4 weeks.

WHEN TO PLANT & SPACING: May–August, 10–40cm (4–16in) for small or large leaves and roots. Seeds are mostly large and each one can grow two or three plants. These vegetables grow well in such clumps. Sow 'Boltardy' beetroot from February indoors and chard from April, then outdoors any time until July; direct sowings need to be thinned to the desired spacing, according to whether you want larger or smaller leaves and roots. Young seedlings are a favourite of sparrows and may need covering with fleece, cloche or wire covers.

Beetroot comes in many colours and makes dishes of great beauty, especially when cut thinly for salads, to expose the moon-rings of different colour – 'Chioggia' in particular. For a full rich beet flavour I recommend any red variety.

CARE: Chard and beets make leaves of great beauty for salads, but when eaten raw the flavour is rather metallic and earthy, so they are best picked frequently as small leaves. Beetroots swell fast once plants are established, and June sowings are excellent for large winter roots to harvest in autumn.

Beetroot 'Boltardy' in June. I sowed four seeds per module indoors in March, planted in April and fleeced the plants for one month.

TIP: Sow late August–early September for indoor winter leaves

JUNE
week 3

How to grow:
COURGETTES

WHERE & WHEN TO SOW: Sow indoors mid-April–May, or outdoors in late May to early June.

TIME FROM SOWING TO PLANTING: 4–5 weeks.

WHEN TO PLANT & SPACING: Mid-May (fleeced) or late May–June, 60–100cm (24–39in).

CARE: To enjoy harvests by midsummer's day, sow indoors around the third week of April, in 5cm (2in) pots: lay a seed flat on top of each, and then push it in gently and cover with 1cm (1/2in) of compost. Plants can be set out when their first true leaf has grown to a fair size, after about three weeks, and a covering of fleece will help them no end. Or you can move plants to a slightly larger pot and keep them indoors for an extra week. Handle plants carefully at every stage, because the roots, stems and leaves are all fragile.

Outdoor sowing needs the warmer soil of mid- to late May, until early June: place two seeds per station and thin to the strongest.

TIP: If you have a glut of courgettes, stop watering the plants temporarily. They go semi-dormant in dry weather and become productive again after rain or watering.

Many leaves and stems have prickly spines, so gloves and a long-sleeved shirt may be useful for picking courgettes. Remove any side shoots of new leaves on the lower stem; otherwise these grow marrows and prevent growth of courgettes at the main growing point.

Courgette plants grow fast and large, so be sure to allow room: up to 1m (39in) in diameter for each plant, depending on variety. They are best planted after soil has been bare for a good month, to reduce slug numbers, or you can plant them on a heap of half-ripe compost or manure. Courgettes need plenty of organic matter, to feed them and conserve moisture. It is worth watering in dry summers – a good soak every week.

Less weeding is needed than for other vegetables because such large and fast-growing plants can smother weeds, but think ahead to next year's sowing and search for hidden weeds, to pull them and prevent any seeding.

Courgettes are prolific in warm summers.

JUNE
week 4

JUNE
Jobs for the month

Use the long days of June to expand your repertoire of garden jobs, from weeding and sowing to staking beans and peas, then pinching out their tops when in full flower. Be ready for some great harvests.

CLEARING: Only a little clearing is needed in June – of spinach, overwintered cabbage and onion and a few salad plants.

WEEDING: As for May; keep the soil clean around all plants and also where sowing or planting is yet to happen.

SOWING INDOORS OR OUTDOORS: Sow kale, purple sprouting broccoli, savoy cabbage, swede and a second batch of lettuce in early June; around or after mid-month is good for winter carrots and beetroot, also bulb fennel and autumn calabrese.

PLANTING: Brussels sprouts, all kinds of summer beans, outdoor cucumber and tomato in early June. Setting out leek and swede plants by month's end will give them time to grow large.

STAKING: Check stakes for peas and broad beans, adding extra support as necessary.

WATERING: Mainly for plants newly set out and for salad plants.

HARVESTING: An exciting month, as the first harvests of beetroot, carrots, potatoes, courgette, calabrese, cauliflower, lettuce hearts, broad beans and peas can all come ready at different moments, and asparagus continues until the last week. The first cucumbers under cover are ready by month's end.

A June harvest of broad beans, asparagus, spinach, cabbage and beetroot.

JULY

JULY boasts the first signs of
abundance as courgettes and
many other spring sowings
begin to produce in large
amounts. Then as soon as any
plants finish cropping, such
as peas, broad beans, spinach
and salads, clear all foliage and
stems (leave roots in the soil)
and immediately sow or plant
kale, broccoli and fennel, as
well as salads for autumn.

Second cropping

What happens to growing areas after the early summer harvests of lettuce, spinach, broad beans, beetroot and so forth? If you can have some plants ready, a second harvest is often possible in the same space and this can be good for the plot, because fewer weeds grow when soil is cropped and there is more incentive to keep weeds at bay, which is of great long-term benefit.

To succeed with succession requires preparation and some precision about dates for sowing and planting, to make best use of diminishing daylight after midsummer. For some second vegetables, it helps to have raised plants in a propagating space for both spring and autumn cropping, so that 3-4 weeks of growing is already done before their roots even meet the soil outside.

Soil preparation between first and second vegetables

Preparing ground for a second planting or sowing is simple when there are few weeds. You just need to clear all surface remains of the first harvest, including any stems just below soil level, but leave all small roots in the soil.

After pulling out roots such as those of cabbage and lettuce, or harvesting garlic, soil is best trodden back down to leave it firm – don't be afraid of walking on undug soil, whose structure should easily take your weight. I find that vegetables grow fine after the soil is trodden down, which also helps to break surface lumps and conserve moisture.

Succeeding through the year

The table below gives ideas of vegetables that can be grown in the first half of the season, and of suitable vegetables to follow them. It is good to have a clear idea of which ones are good in each role.

SOW/PLANT	FIRST VEGETABLE	SOW/PLANT	SECOND VEGETABLE
Aug–Sep	Cabbage for spring	May–Jun	Beans (French and runner); many others
Mar–Apr	Spinach, radish	Jun	Almost any vegetable such as swede, carrot, beans, celery
Oct–Nov	Garlic, broad bean	May–Jul	Kale, cabbage, calabrese
Mar–Apr	Early potato	Jun–Jul	Beans (French and runner), leek (sown April), brassicas
Mar–Apr	Lettuce, carrot, beetroot	Jun–Jul	Dwarf bean, leek, many salads
Mar–Apr	Cauliflower, calabrese, peas	Jul–Aug	Lettuce, endive, chicory
Feb–Apr	Onions	Jul–Aug	Endive, chicory, turnip
Mar–May	Many vegetables	Aug	Oriental leaves, spinach, chervil, coriander, parsley, endive

A great skill to acquire is having plants ready for setting out soon after clearing the first vegetable, even on the same day. This saves up to four weeks of growing time and so effectively extends the season by that amount.

You can also make the growing season longer and increase harvests by covering March and April sowings and plantings with fleece or a cloche, just for a month or so, to propel the vegetables into abundant growth by May.

Many more combinations are possible, according to your climate, skills, facilities and preferences for harvests. I list examples of some of my successions below (1kg equals 2.2lb).

After the spring harvests of different salads from May to early July, I cleared this bed to sow fennel, carrots and plant oriental leaves.

FIRST PLANTING		SECOND PLANTING	
Onion	sown February,* planted March, harvest of 6.3kg early August, from 11 modules of 5 plants in each	Turnips	sown in early August and 3kg harvested by November, from two rows
Beetroot	sown February,* planted March, harvest of 3.1kg in June, from 5 modules of 4 plants in each	Leeks	April sowing outdoors, planted in late June, 3.2kg harvested by December, from 15 plants
Pea, tall sugar snap	sown and planted March, harvest of 8.5kg in late June and July, from 12 modules of 2 plants in each	Endive	module-sown July, planted early August, 1.6kg harvested by November, in several pickings of outer leaves from 5 plants
Lettuce	sown February,* planted March, harvest of 11.3kg April–July from 18 plants of 3 different varieties, their outer leaves picked weekly	Leeks	April sowing outdoors, planted mid-July and 3.3kg harvested by December, from 22 plants
Early potato	planted March, harvest of 4.3kg by mid-June from 4 tubers	Carrots	sown mid-June and 2.7kg harvested October from one row of 1.5m (5ft)
Spinach	sown March, 9.5kg harvested by early June from 2 rows of 1.5m (5ft)	Dwarf beans	planted in early July and 1.2kg harvested by September from 4 plants

* Grown in modules, with some warmth from a propagating bench to germinate seeds, in the greenhouse.

Herbs

Summer salads, with their mild-tasting base of various lettuce varieties, can be given a real zing by the addition of strong-flavoured herbs. Herbs for salads are best picked as young leaves, but when the plants grow larger their leaves can still be used to add flavour to cooked dishes such as omelettes and soups. These are just a few of the best herbs.

Basil

WHERE & WHEN TO SOW: Indoors April–June.

TIME FROM SOWING TO PLANTING: 5–7 weeks.

WHEN TO PLANT & SPACING: Late May–July in shelter; 20–30cm (8–12in)

Sow in trays and prick out seedlings, keeping them in gentle warmth. Water sparingly. Basil is best grown under cover, either direct in the soil or in containers. See page 74 for crop profile.

Chervil

WHERE & WHEN TO SOW: Sow direct or indoors; July–August.

Coriander

TIME FROM SOWING TO PLANTING: 4 weeks.

WHEN TO PLANT & SPACING: August–September, 10–20cm (4–8in); later plantings can be indoors for winter leaves, at 20cm (8in) apart.

Most seed packets advise sowing chervil at any time in spring and summer, but I have found that spring sowing gives minimal harvests before plants flower, whereas summer sowing results in bushy plants which produce abundant, healthy leaves throughout autumn.

Seed can be direct sown, for thinning after 3–4 weeks, or be sown indoors in pots or modules, aiming for 1–3 seedlings in each, for clump planting.

Coriander

WHERE & WHEN TO SOW: Sow indoors April, or direct July–August.

TIME FROM SOWING TO PLANTING: 4 weeks.

WHEN TO PLANT & SPACING: August–September; 15–20cm (6–8in); later plantings indoors for winter leaves.

As with chervil, coriander flowers readily when sown in spring and early summer, but not before some leaves are produced, and the dry seeds of late summer are edible too. Biggest leaf harvests come from late July sowings of, for example, 'Calypso' for picking through autumn, and August sowings to stand the winter. 'Calypso' may provide leaves again in March and April and delicate, tasty white flowers in May.

Seed can be sown direct, or two seeds per module or pot, and thinned to the strongest.

Dill

WHERE & WHEN TO SOW: Sow February indoors, or March outside.

TIME FROM SOWING TO PLANTING: 4 weeks.

WHEN TO PLANT & SPACING: April–June; 20cm (8in).

Dill is a herb for spring and summer, best sown as early as possible to allow time for plenty of leaves to grow and be picked before the plant's energies turn to flowering from late June and through the summer. The flower buds are edible but a little tough.

Parsley

WHERE & WHEN TO SOW: Sow direct March–July, or indoors February–July.

TIME FROM SOWING TO PLANTING: 6–8 weeks.

WHEN TO PLANT & SPACING: April–August, 22cm (9in); later plantings can be indoors for winter leaves.

Parsley germinates and grows slowly at first, even in summer. Seed can be sown as early as February, perhaps in a pot on the windowsill. Two sowings, in March and July, should give leaves for most of the year: plants of a March sowing may grow right through until winter, but are more likely to flower at some point in summer. A summer sowing results in younger plants for winter with more chance of surviving frost.

Sorrel

WHERE & WHEN TO SOW: Sow direct March–July, or indoors February–July.

TIME FROM SOWING TO PLANTING: 4–6 weeks.

WHEN TO PLANT & SPACING: March–August, 25–30cm (10–12in). Later plantings can be indoors for winter leaves.

Sorrel is perennial and may survive many years. You can start a clump or two from roots sliced off an existing plant in winter or from sowing a few of the tiny seeds. Sowing is a useful way of having plants to grow indoors in winter, from sowings into modules or small pots in August, to planting under cover by the end of September as a clump of three or four seedlings. Remove flower stems as they appear from May to July.

Broad-leaved sorrel is the most common variety: buckler-leaved sorrel has smaller leaves, which are tender and tasty in salad, but plants are more likely to die in winter.

Dill

How to grow:
CHICORY/RADICCHIO

WHERE & WHEN TO SOW: Sow indoors June–25 July for plants to form hearts; for chicory for leaves sow direct or indoors June–August.

TIME FROM SOWING TO PLANTING: 3–4 weeks.

WHEN TO PLANT & SPACING: For hearts, July–mid-August, 30–35cm (12–14in): for leaves, late June–August, 10–20cm (4–8in).

CARE: Seeds germinate readily and can be sown indoors in modules or small pots.

Chicory for leaves can be grown closer than hearting chicory, even in clumps. It is more bitter than hearted chicory but easier to grow, from sowings any time in the summer. Cut the leaves with a sharp knife as soon as they are large enough. Cut from the outside of the plant first, so that new leaves will be available from the centre.

Chicory for hearts, usually called radicchio, is slightly more tricky to grow. Plants are more likely to flower than to heart if sown in April, May and even early June, so timing is critical. Plants from a July sowing, set out in August, can follow a harvest of onion, carrot and so forth, making them a most useful second crop vegetable for autumn and winter salads.

Chicory hearts are self blanching to an extent, as the tightly clasping heart leaves cut out light. You can cover the plants with a pot to keep out all light, but this encourages slug damage and can cause leaves to rot.

TIP: Harvests of chicory hearts in November can be stored somewhere cool for salad leaves until January.

Harvest the hearts as soon as they feel firm. Cut them carefully with a sharp knife, leaving a rosette of leaves. Chicory plants will quickly regrow and may even form a new heart again. If not, the leaves that regrow can be used as for leaf chicory.

Chicory 'Castelfranco', with mizuna.

JULY
week 1

How to grow: SUMMER PURSLANE

WHERE & WHEN TO SOW: Sow direct June–July or sow a tiny pinch of seeds per module under cover for planting out.

TIME FROM SOWING TO PLANTING: 3–4 weeks.

SPACING: 15–22cm (6–9in).

CARE: A difficult vegetable unless summer is dry: but it has lovely succulent leaves. It is worth making a small sowing in any spare soil and seeing what grows – hope for sunshine. In hot weather when other salads are flagging, this one is ebullient – indeed it is a weed in many tropical areas and is known as pigweed in North America.

To harvest, cut or pinch 2.5–5cm (1–2in) off its stems when the plant is about 15cm (6in) high. Pick the stems before the formation of any flower buds, which are difficult to see – they are small and of similar colour to the leaves, with a bitter flavour. After the first cut, new stems will keep appearing out of the main one to give a continued season of cropping.

The commonest form of summer purslane is a golden-leaved variety, though the leaves are more yellowish green than truly golden.

TIP: Pick purslane early in the morning for the most succulent leaves, when they are fully charged with moisture from overnight.

How to grow: LAND CRESS

WHERE & WHEN TO SOW: Sow direct or indoors late July–August.

TIME FROM SOWING TO PLANTING: 3–4 weeks.

WHEN TO PLANT & SPACING: August– early September; 20cm (8in).

CARE: Land cress flowers in spring and makes most leaves in autumn and winter from a summer sowing, so most benefit comes from sowing and planting in August, for autumn salad. Seed is small; be careful to sow thinly, either direct or into modules, and thin to one plant.

Harvest leaves when the plants are large enough, either by cutting across the top or by pulling larger leaves from around the edge.

Land cress

TIP: Land cress plants are extremely winter hardy, but pigeons like them even more than we do and some bird cover is usually needed from about October.

How to grow:
ONIONS

WHERE & WHEN TO SOW: Sow seed direct in March, or indoors February–March.

TIME FROM SOWING TO PLANTING: 4–6 weeks.

WHEN TO PLANT & SPACING: April–early May; 25cm (10in). Module plants or sets direct mid-March–mid-April; sets 12cm (5in) or 7 x 25cm (3 x 10in).

CARE: Sow seed of red and white varieties in modules indoors with 6–10 seeds in each, thinned to the 5–6 strongest plants after about three weeks, and planted when still quite small, without thinning. Onions actually like growing together in clumps and their bulbs push one another apart as they swell in early summer.

'Sturon' onions in July. I sowed eight seeds per module indoors in February and planted them outside in early April.

TIP: Sow onions for salad in late August for plants to stand winter and harvest in the spring.

Onions from seed are slow to grow and planting sets is easier (though sets do risk bringing diseases such as mildew or neck rot into your plot). Use a dibber to make holes for the sets and put the fatter end downwards, sometimes with tiny roots just visible and even a green shoot from the top as well. Plant sets only from the third week in March onwards, to avoid them bolting in May and June. If you see a stem with a round flower bud, pull the onion immediately and eat whatever is tender, as there is no point in leaving it to flower.

Grow onions in weed-free soil with a mulch of compost. Water is rarely needed unless the spring is really dry. Warm sun in June and July helps growth and drying.

Onions will be ready to harvest from July until early August. Wait until about half the leaves have fallen over, then pull all bulbs, with their main roots, and leave them on the soil for a few days to dry in the sun and wind. When they are partly dry you can collect them up and spread them out under cover, with the leaves still on and some air around them, to finish drying; or plait or bunch them and hang in an airy spot. Once they are dry, and if not infected with mildew, they should store throughout winter, either indoors or in a shed, even if it is frosty.

JULY
week 3

Versatile vegetables

Some vegetables behave differently according to when they are sown. For example, spinach sown in March or April will rise to flower within 2-3 months, so it is ready to be cleared by June and can be followed by many summer and autumn vegetables.

However, when sown in early August spinach can live for nine months, giving leaves in autumn, surviving the winter and then providing leaves again until the end of May. So it can be used to precede or to follow other crops. Similar examples of altered behaviour are offered by most plants that can survive a winter outdoors, such as some varieties of cabbage, cauliflower, lettuce and onion.

Half-season vegetables

Other vegetables are more predictable and offer a harvest after a half season as either first or second crops. They include beetroot, calabrese, carrot, kohl rabi, lettuce, onion for salad and radish.

Some half-season vegetables show a marked difference as to which half they are best in: for example, broad beans, peas and early potatoes grow relatively poorly in the second half, from a summer sowing, when they suffer more diseases. In contrast, there is a large group that give reliable harvests only in the second half, because spring is their flowering season: these include bulb fennel, chervil, chicory, endive, land cress, turnips and oriental vegetables in general, including Chinese cabbage, mizuna, mustards, pak choi and tatsoi.

Winter harvests

Kale and broccoli are a must for tasty pickings all through autumn, winter and early spring, and they grow well from sowing in June, to plant in July or early August after clearing other crops.

Kale needs netting from pigeons in winter but is worth that extra effort because it makes new leaves at lower temperatures than most other crops, and survives much frost. For broccoli, choose a variety that makes shoots in the season you want to eat them.

You can also grow perennial broccoli from seed and perennial kale from plants: Daubenton kale is particularly productive, and is easy to propagate from its many shoots, just dibbed into damp soil.

Knowing how crops behave and how long they take to reach full production can help to make a plot far more productive by being used all year round.

Taking on an allotment

If you have too little suitable space at home, taking on ground at an allotment is a logical step. Before committing to it, reflect on how many spare hours you can give to a project such as this. Remember to add in the time you will need to spend walking or driving to reach the allotment, as it may be quite a distance from your home.

My two main pieces of advice are to consider sharing an allotment, and to look closely at what you are offered before accepting it.

Allotment sharing

Sharing offers mutual support and reduces the size of a plot to a more manageable level. Allotments were created for large families, growing serious amounts of food. Vegetables were relatively expensive, so there were stronger financial incentives to grow them than there are now.

If you have time and want to be self-sufficient in potatoes, cauliflower and onions, then a whole allotment is worth attempting. If your time is limited and you want mainly salads, green beans and courgettes, a quarter of an allotment is probably sufficient to take on.

Checking the plot

Another reason for plot sharing is that, before handover to new holders, many allotment plots have suffered neglect, which allows large numbers of weeds to grow that are difficult to keep on top of and need to be patiently cleared before you start growing. For example, I have seen allotments where couch grass is established everywhere, and it may need a full year of a light-excluding mulch to try to get rid of it before you can start planting. A smaller plot is far less daunting than a whole one when weeds need to be cleared.

If you decide to go ahead with an allotment, you will first need to contact your local council to apply for a plot. It is quite likely that your name will have to be added to a waiting list, as in many areas there are not enough allotments to go round. Sometimes alternative allotments are provided by private landlords; contact your local allotment society for more information.

This plot was barren ten years ago with compacted soil. It was remedied simply by putting organic matter on top.

JULY
Jobs for the month

Already there will be harvests finishing such as salads, carrot, beetroot, spinach, peas, overwintered broad beans, garlic and shallots. As soon as the last picking is done, clear all debris and weeds (there should be few weeds) and firm soil with your feet – gently if wet, with full weight if dry – and then plant straight away with plants you have raised or bought.

WEEDING: In dry summers there may be fewer weeds, but keep your eyes open because a few weeds setting seed causes much more work for years to come; also have a search for weeds under large leaves of courgettes, beans and brassicas.

COMPOSTING: Spread 1cm ($^1/_2$in) only on soil that has none left on top. Do this either before new sowings and plantings or, later, around plants that are already growing.

SOWING INDOORS OR OUTDOORS: Sow lettuce for autumn, other autumn/winter salads such as endive and chicory, and parsley to overwinter.

PLANTING: Kale, swede, savoy cabbage, cauliflower, purple sprouting, beetroot in early July; also bulb fennel and calabrese.

WATERING: In dry weather most value comes from watering salads and all larger plants that are flowering and cropping such as French and runner beans and courgettes.

HARVESTING: July is an abundant time after June's hint of summer feasts: potatoes, peas, broad beans and courgettes may be especially fruitful; globe artichokes come ready; and garlic wants lifting by early July, to dry and be stored; also shallots.

Globe artichokes in midsummer. The plants are fourteen years old and die back every winter.

AUGUST

There are still great sowings
to make at this late stage,
including the beautiful,
multiflavoured oriental leaves
and quick-cropping radishes.
Harvest potatoes in AUGUST
before blight takes a hold, and
onions too. Water occasionally
and plentifully rather than
little and often, and go looking
for weeds that will be hiding
among your vegetables, to hoe
or remove them before they
drop hundreds of seeds.

Tackling pests and diseases

All pests have times of year when they are most numerous and active: aphids and flea beetles in spring; moths and midges in summer and autumn; red spider mite in warm, dry conditions; slugs in wet ones. Knowing each pest's preferences can help avoid them overrunning our plants, chiefly by timing sowings to make plants' main growth happen when problems are less likely.

Below are some guidelines to keep in the back of your mind when you are growing vegetables, with the aim of reducing damage. Remember that pests are almost always present, in small numbers we hope; otherwise their predators could not be.

Sow in the right season

The presence and impact of pests, or lack of them, are often a result of sowing and planting at a certain time. For example, leeks planted too late are at risk of suffering badly from leek moth; brassicas planted too early in the spring can be clobbered by flea beetles; and courgettes planted when it is too cold are often eaten by slugs. Growing healthy vegetables is a precise act: the dates suggested in this book aim to give best growth and fewest problems.

Sowing in the right season means plants encounter conditions in which they can achieve robust and often rapid growth, with fewer problems around them, as well as having more ability to grow away from any problems they meet. Compare runner beans sown in April, growing feebly and with slugs often eating any small leaves, with a later sowing in June when the extra warmth enables rapid growth, so that the very same slugs are barely interested.

Sometimes you can 'switch season' to avoid pests. If, for instance, your cabbage hearts are often holed by caterpillars, try growing spring cabbage sown in late summer, for harvesting in April and May, so avoiding the times when butterflies are on the wing. Where potato blight is a common problem, grow earlies instead of maincrop, so that they have done their growing before the arrival of midsummer blight.

Sow in the best conditions

For healthiest growth, give seeds and seedlings their favourite temperature and environment. These normally occur when you sow at the right time, but sometimes it also helps to sow seeds in a protected environment: seedlings in general are more vulnerable to pests than large plants, and certain seedlings have special difficulties. For instance, small leaves of beetroot are adored by birds and woodlice, so I advise sowing beetroot in modules under cover, for planting out when established; swede can be difficult to raise outdoors but grows well from an indoor sowing, which affords protection against flea beetles eating its leaves.

Grow resistant plants

Some crops in general are more prone to pests than others. Brassicas, for example, are frequently attacked by flea beetles in spring and caterpillars in summer to early autumn; they are also prone to damage from cabbage root flies from April to August. Carrots are similarly damaged by carrot root flies in both early summer and autumn.

Leeks used to be one of the easier vegetables to grow, but there has recently been a rapid increase of leek moth from France. The moth's caterpillars are small but they eat the plants' most tender leaves right in the middle, causing a severe reduction in growth and even the destruction of small leeks.

Sometimes there are varieties known to cope with certain problems that may be common in your area. I have found that 'Grenoble Red' lettuces are less tempting to slugs than other varieties; red lettuces succumb to more mildew than green ones but suffer less from slug damage; savoy cabbages cope better with caterpillars than ballheads; and Sarpo potatoes resist blight well, although taste and texture are variable. On the other hand, I am not convinced by the performance of supposedly root-fly-resistant carrots!

Cabbage white caterpillars on kale. The damage looks bad, but healthy plants will recover.

How to grow:
RADISHES

WHERE & WHEN TO SOW: For an autumn harvest, sow direct late July–mid-August. For a spring and summer harvest, sow direct March–May.

SPACING: For summer-sown crops, thin after three weeks to 5 x 30cm (2 x 12in). Spring-sown crops should be thinned after one month to 1 x 25cm (½ x 10in).

CARE: Radish seed germinates fast and easily. Sow the seeds direct and thin the seedlings; if left too thick, roots struggle to develop. Keep the plants moist as they develop; if grown in dry conditions the roots can become woody in texture and unpleasantly hot in flavour. Pull the young roots as soon as they are large enough to eat; do not leave them to get old and coarse.

For autumn harvests, sow the larger pink, black and white varieties such as 'Minnowase'.

For spring sowing, use small, red or red-and-white varieties ('French Breakfast'); they can be sown between or even in rows of slow-germinating seedlings such as parsnips, or around vegetables that are about to finish, such as winter salads.

Radishes for leaves

Although the leaves are often thrown on the compost heap when radishes are trimmed, they are perfectly edible. They have a mild, peppery radish taste; they are mainly used in salads but can also be cooked and are widely used in Indian cuisine. The leaves of any variety can be used, but the mooli or Japanese radish is

TIP: Radishes can also be grown as micro-leaves for salads all round the year; grow them indoors just like mustard and cress. The variety 'Sangria' has been specially developed for this use and is particularly attractive with its rosy red stems.

probably the favourite type to grow for salad leaves. The leaves grow extremely fast in autumn, and if you do not pick them too hard you may also harvest a long white root of mooli radish by October. Plants survive moderate frost and can make it to Christmas if autumn is mild.

'Cherry Belle' round radish.

Green manures

Growing green manures between harvests of vegetables is a way of keeping soil covered and maintaining fertility. Consequently there will be less need to import organic matter, as long as the ground is not required for growing food (a major caveat: see below). Sowings of clover, phacelia, buckwheat and grazing rye can be effective in large plots, sown after growing one vegetable per season, and if digging is done as part of soil preparation, incorporating them will not be extra work. Compared to spreading bought-in compost and manure, green manures are sometimes a cheaper, simpler and less resource-intensive way of slightly enriching soil.

Persian clover (*Trifolium resupinatum*) and mustard (*Brassica juncea*) both grow fast and are killed by frost of about −7°C/19°F or lower, so there is no need to smother or incorporate them. The former can be sown from July to August and the latter from August to early September, but only if you are not wanting to sow any more vegetables at those times. Persian clover is a relatively new crop in Britain but has been grown with success in other countries with a similar climate. It is quick growing and soon produces a thick cover of leaves.

I recommend weeding these green manures in exactly the same way as if they were plants for eating.

Lupins are perennial and feed the soil.

Green manure alternative

In a small plot, where the aim is to enjoy harvests as much of the time as possible, often through second cropping, there is not room for green manures. It is simpler and more productive to buy the relatively small amount of additional organic matter needed to maintain fertility, spread it in late autumn and grow vegetables continuously throughout the season. This is more effective than sowing a green manure that will need to be dug in, will remove nutrients from growing crops while it is decomposing and will offer a habitat for slugs and opportunities for new weeds, because of both digging and weeds going to seed during the growth of the green manure.

AUGUST
week 1

How to grow:
ORIENTAL LEAVES & ROCKET

WHERE & WHEN TO SOW: Sow direct or indoors July–August (early August is best).

TIME FROM SOWING TO PLANTING: 2–3 weeks.

WHEN TO PLANT & SPACING: August–early September; 15–22cm (6–9in).

CARE: All these plants are best sown after midsummer, to avoid their spring flowering season. I find that July sowings suffer from pests such as flea beetle and caterpillars more than August sowings, which are better placed to enjoy the dampness of autumn. Sowings in the first two weeks of August give the most productive harvests, and I restrict sowings in late August to the fastest-growing plants – mizuna, leaf radish, 'Green in the Snow' mustard and salad rocket.

All these seeds can be sown in modules with two to four seeds, depending how many plants you want in a clump; fewer plants means larger leaves. Sowing direct works well too, with satisfyingly rapid germination.

Varieties

Oriental leaves include pak choi, tatsoi, mizuna, mibuna, leaf radish and mustards of many colours. Sowings from a pack of mixed seeds will show you their range of growth and flavours: my favourite is 'Red Frills' mustard.

Rocket is actually two different vegetables – salad and wild. August sowings of salad rocket and oriental leaves will produce healthy leaves

TIP: Sow mid- to late September for indoor winter leaves.

through autumn, possibly surviving winter too and giving a new flush of leaves and stems in March and April, by which time the plants will be eight months old. Regular picking helps plants to live longer, until May; cutting leaves is also possible.

Wild rocket is perennial, slower growing than the other plants here, so I sow it in July for harvests in both autumn and right through spring until it flowers in July. It has thinner, more serrated leaves with a stronger flavour than salad rocket.

September: Salad rocket and 'Red Dragon' mustard were sown six weeks earlier.

How to grow:
ENDIVE

WHERE & WHEN TO SOW: Sow indoors June–July (for hearts); sow direct or indoors June–August (for leaves).

TIME FROM SOWING TO PLANTING: 3–4 weeks.

WHEN TO PLANT & SPACING: For hearts, July–August, 30–35cm (12–14in); for leaves, June–September, 20–25cm (8–10in).

CARE: One of the easier seeds to germinate, and only a few plants are needed, but beware of slugs in the fortnight after setting out young plants. Seedlings grow well after being pricked out, so I sow clumps of seeds in a pot or tray for pricking into modules or small pots.

TIP: Sow leaf endive from late August to early September, for indoor winter leaves.

Endive comes in two main forms: frisée, with thin, serrated leaves; or scarole, with thicker and larger leaves. Both can be sown from June to August, with the possibility of huge plants, but there comes a point where leaf quality deteriorates as the edges go brown, so it is best to cut out the hearts when they are of fair size and slightly blanched. This is likely to be about ten weeks from sowing on average. After early autumn harvests, a second cut is possible.

Endive is a most underrated autumn and winter salad. You can make leaves of large salads such as endives less bitter by blanching – depriving them of light for a week or two. This can be done by gathering the leaves together and tying with string, or by placing an upturned pot over the plants. However, this can cause some leaves to rot and encourage extra slugs: you may find it simpler to sweeten the salad dressing instead! Plants grown for their hearts are naturally self blanching.

Frisée endives such as 'Frenzy' can be sown until early August.

AUGUST
week 3

How to grow:
CABBAGES

For spring leaves & hearting cabbages

WHERE & WHEN TO SOW: Sow indoors or outdoors mid- to late August.

TIME FROM SOWING TO PLANTING: 4–5 weeks.

WHEN TO PLANT & SPACING: Second half of September; 20cm (8in) for leaves and 40cm (16in) for hearts.

CARE: Seeds can be sown in pots or trays under cover, or in rows in a nursery bed outdoors. Seed is often of variable quality, so when sown in a pot or tray I prick out only the strongest seedlings, or plant only the strongest plants from an outdoor row. For spring cabbage, plants need to be in the soil before the end of September, so that they have time to establish before winter.

All cabbages like an open and sunny site and rich, moisture-retentive soil. The weather is often dry at planting time, so water the new plants in generously. Like all brassicas cabbages are prone to a variety of pests and diseases, though one of the worst brassica pests, the cabbage caterpillar, is far more of a problem on summer crops than winter and spring ones. Over winter you will find that pigeons are likely to be a major nuisance, but plants can be protected by netting suspended on stakes. Make sure it is held about 45cm (18in) above the plants or the birds will simply land on top and peck through the net.

For autumn & winter hearting cabbages

WHERE & WHEN TO SOW: Sow indoors or outdoors May–early June.

TIME FROM SOWING TO PLANTING: 4–6 weeks.

WHEN TO PLANT & SPACING: June–mid-July; 45–50cm (18–20in).

By late May, 'Derby Day' cabbage, spaced at 38cm (15in), is almost ready to harvest.

TIP: When harvesting cabbages, leave the stump in the ground and cut a shallow cross in the top of it. Within a few weeks a fresh cluster of small, leafy heads will be produced.

When to water

At this time of year the weather may be very dry, and watering can be necessary in some instances, especially for salads. Plants in soil that has not been dug and with a good compost mulch on the surface are unlikely to need more than an occasional watering, but when watering is needed it is most effective when done thoroughly and with several days between waterings.

At sowing times

Sowing in summer is often in dry soil, and this can actually result in better germination than when soil is consistently wet, by using the following method.

Draw your drill or drills slightly deeper than usual, about 2.5cm (1in), and then run a watering can slowly along their length so that water fills the drill without overflowing its sides. If soil is really dry, it is good to do this two or three times.

The idea is for seeds to lie on this damp soil and send their roots down into it. Above them is dry soil, which you pull back over once the seeds are sown. 'Sow in dust, grow they must' – the soil looks dry, but there is moisture where it is really needed.

Avoid the temptation to water the soil at any stage for at least three weeks, until seedlings are established, and they should be troubled with fewer weeds and slugs than usual, because of the dry soil.

New plants

In dry weather, new plants need watering precisely rather than massively.

Watering soil thoroughly before planting.

I find that using a long-handled dibber gives enough leverage to make reasonably deep holes in dry soil, with a slight hollow around each plant, making it possible to give small amounts of water where most needed, just around new plants and not over the whole area. Precise watering of sowings and plantings saves much water, and means fewer weeds grow.

Containers

Plants in containers will need more watering than plants in open soil. Sometimes it can be difficult to judge when container plants need watering as the compost can look wet on top while it is bone dry underneath. If you are unsure, try lifting the container to see if it is light or heavy – this will give a better idea of whether extra water is needed.

Tackling potato
and tomato blight

The fungal disease blight is evolving and becoming ever harder to avoid, as it infects varieties of potato and tomato that previously had some resistance. Your best approach is to learn when blight can appear and how to keep plants healthy when it does.

Late blight

There are two kinds of blight, of which late blight (*Phytopthora infestans*) is the most harmful, because it multiplies fast in moist summer weather. Large, healthy plants of potato and tomato can turn to a brown, rotting mess within a week. Literally as soon as you see the first translucent patches of fungal damage, during spells of wet weather from late June to September, you should cut potato stems to the ground and harvest tubers either then or soon, when convenient. Also prune any blighted leaves off tomato plants.

However, once any plants are infected, the blight fungus travels through stems to fruit so harvests can be marginal. The only remedy is to keep leaves dry, so that the spores that abound in moist, warm air cannot

establish and breed on your plants. For tomatoes under cover you need to water plants at soil level only.

For potatoes, the best method is to plant rapid-growing second early varieties such as 'Charlotte', which give worthwhile harvests before blight arrives.

You may compost all leaves, stems and fruits infected with late blight, as the fungus cannot survive without a host of living tissue. I regularly compost blighted material and have spread this compost where I then plant tomatoes, with no ill effects.

Early blight

Less harmful and more rare is early blight (*Alternaria solani*), which survives on infected potatoes left deep enough in the soil to escape destruction by frost. Early blight then appears on leaves growing from these tubers, with brown patches on leaves and eventual rotting of stems, but you can still have a harvest of tubers as the blight damages them so slowly.

Blight on tomatoes, causing both leaves and stems to rot, and then the fruit.

AUGUST
week 4

AUGUST
Jobs for the month

Clearing continues this month as you continue to remove any crop residues in order to sow or plant again, often on the same day: for example, sow turnips after clearing onions; or sow land cress after early French beans have finished.

WEEDING: As for July, in dry summers there may be fewer weeds, but keep your eyes open because a few weeds setting seed cause much more work for years to come; also have a search for weeds under large leaves of courgettes, beans and brassicas.

COMPOSTING: Do this possibly before planting autumn salads.

SOWING INDOORS OR OUTDOORS: Oriental leaves, rocket, coriander and chervil are best sown in early August, also spinach and chard to overwinter; then land cress and winter purslane mid-month, followed by overwintering cabbage, onions and lettuce in the last week; also lamb's lettuce at month's end, for harvesting from November, and salads for planting in September to grow under a cloche through winter.

PLANTING: Chicory for radicchio in early August, endive, rocket, oriental leaves, chervil, coriander, spinach, chard.

WATERING: As for July; well-composted soil needs less water than usual, and you can save water when sowing seeds in dry soil by watering only the bottom of the drill, so that seeds fall on moist soil but are then covered with dry soil.

HARVESTING: A season of gluts is possible, of runner and French beans, tomatoes, courgettes, cucumber; also onions and potatoes to store.

Keep picking cucumbers when young and tender.

SEPTEMBER

The first hints of autumn
belie SEPTEMBER's excellent
harvests of summer vegetables
such as beans, courgettes and
tomatoes. You can help the
ripening of tomatoes grown
undercover by halving the
water given, and keeping
leaves on the plants' top half.
Garlic is good to plant now.

Seed saving tips

Saving your own seed is a great way of ensuring good germination, although it requires extra space in the garden, as well as time and a little homework, to find out the different methods and timings for each vegetable. I offer some advice here, based on my own experience.

- A golden rule is not to save seed from F1 hybrids, because it will be a mix of different varieties, mostly undesirable.
- For some vegetables you need to be careful of cross-pollination by insects, which may be carrying pollen of different varieties in your own or neighbours' plots.
- With biennials, save seed from plants in their second summer. Biennials are plants that grow for a year or part year, overwinter either in leaf (chard, kale, leek) or as a dormant root (parsnip, onion) before sending up a flowering stem in spring, with seed drying through summer.
- Do not save seed from, for example, chard or beetroot that have flowered ('bolted') in the same year as sowing, because the plants have not passed through a winter before flowering and therefore when sown the seed will be more likely to grow into bolters, rather than make chard leaves or beetroots.

Peas

Seed from peas is easy to save as long as you have space to allow a plant (or two), sown before the end of April, to remain unpicked and then to stay in the ground until August, when its pods should be dry and crackling. Pick all the larger, well-formed pods, shell out the peas and keep them warm until you are sure that all are fully dry and hard.

Tomatoes

Like peas, tomatoes rarely cross-pollinate and offer seed as part of their harvest. Choose a healthy, good-sized, fully ripe tomato, cut out some of its seeds and wash them in water before drying on cardboard.

Squash & courgette

Squash and courgette (not F1 hybrid courgette) need more care when saving seed to prevent it being an undesirable combination of different types of cucurbit. You should choose and watch a healthy courgette or squash fruit before its flower opens, rub a male flower of the same plant on the fruit's flower as soon as it does open and then seal the flower with a paper bag held on with a rubber band, until the flower withers, so that it cannot receive any more pollen. (Female flowers have a little swelling at the base of the flower, which will turn into the fruit. Male flowers have no swelling at all on the flower stalk.)

Mark the fruit and leave it unpicked until mature. It should contain many seeds of the same variety.

Lettuce

One long season of steady growth, from a March or April sowing, is needed to make lettuce heart in June and July and then develop a flower bud, which needs staking when about 1m (39in) high; tufts of white seed will be ready to be rubbed out by September. Growing a plant under cover is a sure way of having seed by the end of August, and you should find that home-saved lettuce seed has noticeably more vigour than any you buy.

Garlic

This is saved as bulbs rather than seed. Set aside the largest and healthiest at harvest time for planting its cloves in early autumn.

Rubbing out seeds from a lettuce plant that was allowed to flower in summer.

STORING SEED SAFELY

Once you have harvested your seed, you need to make sure it is completely dry before storing it, otherwise it may rot or start to germinate prematurely. In humid conditions spreading seeds out in an airy, warm place to dry may not work well enough, but you can use a dessicant such as charcoal or dried rice to draw moisture out of the seeds. Place a layer of dessicant in the base of a sealable container, put a thin sheet of newspaper or similar porous material over the top, and spread the seeds on this. Seal the container and leave for about two weeks. After this the seed can be transferred to bags and stored in an airtight container to prevent them reabsorbing moisture from the atmosphere.

SEPTEMBER
week 1

How to grow:
GARLIC

WHERE & WHEN TO PLANT: Plant cloves direct late September to March (early plantings give larger harvests); 15cm (6in) in blocks or 10 x 30cm (4 x 12in) in rows.

CARE: Autumn plantings allow garlic extra time to grow because, whether planted in autumn or early spring, garlic bulbs up in the lengthening daylight of early summer, for harvesting by early July. Plants are completely frost hardy. Break the bulbs into separate cloves and keep any small ones for eating. Use a dibber to make holes for the cloves, and insert with their fatter end downwards. Cover with 2.5–5cm (1–2in) of soil. Or plant cloves less deep and spread compost or manure on the whole bed after planting.

Be patient when waiting for growth to be visible, as they put down a lot of roots first and sometimes you see no leaves until January, even February, from an autumn planting.

Companion plantings

Vegetables that taste good together are often good companions while in growth: for example, garlic can be grown with parsley under cover in winter. Plant parsley in September at its usual spacing of 25–30cm (10–12in) and then plant garlic cloves between the small parsley plants in late September or October. They will all survive winter together and you can pick parsley from February to May, then pull it out when rising to flower, leaving the garlic to mature in early July. I grow some enormous cloves this way, as garlic enjoys the extra warmth from being under cover.

Polytunnel garlic late June, and melon plant growing fast.

TIP: Garlic is saved as bulbs rather than seed. Set aside your largest and healthiest bulb at harvest time and use it for planting in early autumn, separating it into cloves.

When sowing early broad beans, mice can be a problem because they love to devour the seeds. Soaking the seeds overnight in water with a crushed clove of garlic can save the seeds from being eaten.

How to grow:
LAMB'S LETTUCE

WHERE & WHEN TO SOW: For winter leaves, lamb's lettuce is best sown direct in late August or early September.

SPACING: Sow in a row and thin to 5–10cm (2–4in).

CARE: Lamb's lettuce (also known as corn salad) is probably the hardiest outdoor winter salad, as long as you take care to time your sowings well. If sown before mid-August, plants mature in October and November and are at risk of mildew. Sowings made in the damper weather of late August and early September stand the most chance of reaching a fair size as well as staying healthy over winter.

Draw out drills quite close together, about 15–20cm (6–8in) apart. Sow the seeds about 2.5cm (1in) apart and thin after a month if necessary. Unless your soil is clean you will need to weed carefully, because germination is slow and in weedy soils you risk seeing the small plants smothered.

TIP: Although lamb's lettuce is very hardy and does not need protection to keep growing, a covering of glass or polythene suspended above the plants helps to keep the leaves clean and free from soil splashes. Ensure the sides are open so that plenty of air circulates round the plants, otherwise they may develop mildew.

Cut for eating when plants are about 7–10cm (3–4in) in diameter – this is a cold and fiddly job in winter. Cut a little higher than any visible rosettes coming out of the main stem to enable regrowth of smaller heads. You can increase the quality and size of winter harvests by covering plants with fleece from December.

Lamb's lettuce has soft, tender and succulent leaves with a 'melt-in-the-mouth' texture. They have a pleasant, mild flavour. There are a number of different varieties available; 'Vit' is said to have some mildew resistance and 'Cavallo' has large, deep green leaves.

October: Lamb's lettuce 'Pulsar' was sown between French beans in August, for picking from October.

SEPTEMBER
week 2

Growing salads in containers

Salads are an excellent vegetable for growing in small spaces and containers, with the potential for quick harvests of many flavours over a long period. Containers are especially useful in winter, as they can be brought indoors to encourage some growth of salads such as lettuce, endive, chicory, oriental leaves, spinach, winter purslane, land cress and salad onion. When placed on a windowsill through winter, turned fortnightly to give light to the other side, container-grown plants will produce a fair number of leaves from September sowings or plantings, until plants rise to flower in March and April – and the flowers are edible too.

Compost for containers

Your own garden compost should be good to use when a year old and well broken down. Put some in a bucket first and pull out any woody pieces; then add some sharp sand for good drainage and a couple of handfuls of blood, fish and bonemeal for extra nutrients. Multipurpose compost is easy to use and you can grow plenty of leaves in it before feeding becomes necessary.

A lovely winter salad grown under cover in mushroom boxes filled with compost.

How many plants?

Few plants are needed in a container, so if you don't want to grow your own from seed you could buy some. A mushroom crate of 30 x 40cm (12 x 16in) needs six plants, while a 25cm (10in) pot can fit one or two. In larger containers I recommend the same spacing as in a bed: an average of 22cm (9in) between plants, whether single or in clumps.

Feeding & watering

The need for water is often hard to judge because surface compost of outdoor containers, in damp but not really wet weather, can look wet on top and be bone dry underneath. When unsure, lift the container: sometimes you will find it surprisingly light and this means you need to water! Do so in gradual stages, every minute or so, allowing water to soak in rather than run through the dry compost.

After a couple of months, some outer leaves may show signs of yellow, blue and purple, indicating that some feeding is necessary with a general-purpose liquid feed.

Growing
under cover

An indoor growing space is anywhere sheltered from wind and rain, and not necessarily frost-free. Raising plants on a windowsill is a good place to start with indoor growing, then you could try using a coldframe or patio lean-to structure, with a polytunnel or greenhouse worth aspiring to for a place to protect you and your plants from inclement weather.

Any walk-in structure allows you to do a lot of gardening when it is wet and windy; if you have enough space and money, such a structure can prove invaluable. Once you have succeeded with some outdoor crops, a polytunnel or greenhouse is an exciting next step for growing tender and out-of-season vegetables, propagation of small plants, drying onions and garlic, and as a general storage space. If you use any of the following structures for raising plants I suggest fitting them out with some kind of wooden staging.

Greenhouses

Although expensive, greenhouses mostly admit more light and retain more heat than polythene structures, and are especially good for raising plants. Be careful of opening roof vents in wet summer weather, in case you allow blight to infect tomatoes.

Polytunnels

These are much less expensive than greenhouses and come in an infinite range of widths and lengths. I find the cheaper standard polythene is good but bear in mind that it needs replacing every 5–7 years. Look for a structure with easy-to-open doors. Keep edges completely weed-free to deter slugs.

Other options

Cheaper still are lean-to plastic shelters for placing beside a house wall, and they are good value. Where space for a structure is limited, you could use a portable 'mini-greenhouse' on wheels. It is often sold as a kit with shelving included. I would recommend one of these ahead of a cold frame, which takes up extra room and is all at ground level, and is therefore cooler, with plants at more risk of slug damage.

A polytunnel, 4.25m (14ft) wide, with cucumber and tomato in the middle bed, and basil and aubergines in side beds.

Using organic matter

Simple methods work best. Organic matter on the surface is a copy of how things work in nature, where man is not involved: decomposing organic matter lies on top of the soil, decays and then 'disappears', taken into the soil by different organisms.

The problem with transferring this model to vegetable growing is that gardens do not happen in nature. We are creating a somewhat unnatural environment, with more bare soil than usual. Even organic vegetables, in this sense, are 'unnatural'.

Permaculturists solve this problem by creating gardens without bare soil and full of perennial vegetables, bushes and trees. However, in such a garden it is difficult to grow annual vegetables such as carrots, parsnips and lettuce, so you still need a patch of clear ground for growing these. Also the range of perennial vegetables, although interesting, is neither extensive nor likely to feed you for long periods from small areas.

To grow annual vegetables continuously in the same ground, a weed-free surface is essential: initially, to have successful germination with fewer pests around, and later for growth to be abundant without the competition of weeds.

I suggest that treating bare, undug soil with surface mulches of compost is a way of replicating nature's principles, if not methods, effectively using the composting process as a shortcut. This means there is organic matter on the surface, which is suitable for sowing and planting vegetables into. The unnatural environment of soil that is bare for some of the year is compensated by compost providing food and undisturbed shelter for all its organisms. Once vegetables are growing, their leaves cover the soil and nature is assuaged. This is the easy time in vegetable growing. The more tricky part can be managing a plot when it is empty, and this is where compost plays a key role.

Enriching the surface all the time

In my garden I am often asked why the soil level is not rising, because of my annual spreading of 2.5–5cm (1–2in) compost on the beds. I suggest that without such additions the soil level would actually descend. I can see this in a polytunnel where I add 5cm (2in) of compost and manure every spring, yet the level inside is no higher than the level of soil under the grass on the plastic's outer side, where the growing and decaying of grass and its roots is a similar continuous cycle of soil maintenance and improvement.

Organic matter on the surface benefits all kinds of wildlife. The soil food chain is strengthened with extra bacteria, fungi, grubs, worms and beetles among other soil inhabitants. These soil inhabitants provide regular food for more visible members of the above-ground food chain such as birds, hedgehogs, slow worms, badgers and even slugs and snails. All play a role in helping to maintain a healthy, humming balance of life and of nutrients for growing plants.

Does organic matter need to be incorporated?

Digging compost and manure into the soil, as often recommended, is called incorporation. The supposed idea is that doing so places organic matter 'closer to plant roots'. But, as well as shattering the existing soil structure, this ignores the fact that most plants root extensively in the top few centimetres. For example, just below surface level, when the soil is moist, I find fibrous roots of courgette, salad, chard, chicory and spinach. Parsnips too! It is therefore baffling to me that so many gardeners eschew the benefits of spreading organic matter on top. Similarly, when planting trees, fill the hole with soil only and then mulch with organic matter.

When soil life is undisturbed and allowed to 'get busy' with organic matter on the surface, an undug area

WHEN TO SPREAD COMPOST
Any time of year is possible, for instance when using compost as a mulch around established plants. Less-rotted compost can be for mulching larger vegetables in early summer, or for spreading after a final harvest in autumn, to finish breaking down in surface air.

If there is a clear choice, spreading in autumn gives best results: the soil is usually moist and warm enough then for organisms to busy themselves with feeding on the new goodies and to distribute them widely. Then the compost is broken down by winter weather, becoming soft and more friable by spring.

has plenty of nutrients at a greater depth, without them having to be put there by digging, because the soil inhabitants are continually moving them around and incorporating them more efficiently than we ever can.

Mature compost, eight months old. I turned the heap once.

Tackling
slugs and snails

In dry conditions, slugs may not be a problem, but in warm, continually moist weather their numbers increase rapidly, and they forage more hungrily and further. Their favourite foods include salad leaves, brassicas, carrot seedlings and roots, potato tubers and beetroot. Some vegetables suffer little damage – alliums in particular.

Here I use the word 'slug' to embrace snails as well; most gardeners have to contend with both at some point. In my garden, on clay soil and in a damp climate, much of what I do is influenced by the need to keep their population at a manageable level. Since they are always present, or potentially present, I strive to reduce their likely habitats.

TIP: Slug habitats include weeds, old and decaying leaves, long grass, walls and piles of stone, and any spots that are consistently damp and dark.

Slugs are most interested in outer leaves, which are decaying anyway.

Vulnerable plant parts

The most eaten parts of a plant are the oldest and sometimes the most tender, rather than strongly growing, mid-plant leaves. Tidying the garden by removing older, decaying leaves is a good precaution, in order to reduce possible hiding places for slugs and to help the soil surface become dry after rain has cleared. Wooden sides of raised beds are also a habitat for slugs, and you will need to check these regularly.

Where I have experimented with dug and undug beds, I have tended to find more slug damage on the dug beds, where I have needed to replace more slug-damaged plants every season than on the undug beds. Slugs find it easier to slither over the surface of the dug soil; compost lying on the undug soil surface is rougher and contains twigs, making it less attractive to slugs because it is harder to travel over.

TIP: Slugs in salads can be reduced by frequent picking of small to medium sized leaves, so that there are few if any larger leaves for slugs to live under.

centipedes and beetles. Deterrents such as soot, sand, gravel, salt and garlic need to be used with care – many plants do not like salty soil and too much gravel dilutes good soil and compost. Soot, sand and ash lose efficacy after rain.

'Organic' slug pellets of ferrophosphate are a milder poison. These are best used in moderation and kept for extreme conditions and the most vulnerable plants; likewise nematodes, which are effective but expensive, are wasted if the weather is dry after you apply them.

Protective measures

Wet weather can see slug numbers and activity increase dramatically. When this happens, it is worth venturing out at dusk or dawn with a torch to see exactly what is going on, and you may be surprised at their numbers. I take a pointed knife to skewer them, or you can put them into a bucket for later disposal – hens like snails above all.

Container plants are often vulnerable, with slug habitats nearby or underneath. A copper strip around the container can deter them, but make sure that no leaves are growing over it, providing an entry point. Hunt around your containers, especially underneath any dark, damp objects, for lurking slugs.

Trapping slugs is effective but needs time, and in doing so you also catch

KEEPING SLUGS AWAY FROM TENDER SEEDLINGS

- Sow each vegetable in its right season, so that young plants are strong enough to grow despite the occasional nibble.

- When sowing indoors, keep your propagating space clear of slug habitats and check any damp, dark spaces for slugs.

- Sow outdoors in clean, bare soil, not close to overgrowing weeds or plants whose leaves are draping on to the soil. Slugs are another reason to keep weeds to an absolute minimum, to reduce damp habitats.

How to grow:
WINTER PURSLANE

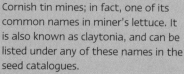

WHERE & WHEN TO SOW: Sow direct or indoors, early to mid-August, or in September for winter leaves under cover.

TIME FROM SOWING TO PLANTING: 4 weeks.

WHEN TO PLANT & SPACING: Plant by mid-September; 15–22cm (6–9in)

CARE: Winter purslane is a great standby for mild-flavoured winter salads, from sowings in late summer. It thrives only in cool and damp weather. Growing wild in moist, mild areas it was an invaluable source of winter and spring vitamin C for miners in the Californian gold rush and the

A salad of winter purslane and radicchio.

Cornish tin mines; in fact, one of its common names in miner's lettuce. It is also known as claytonia, and can be listed under any of these names in the seed catalogues.

Winter purslane seeds are tiny, and it is easy to sow them too thickly. Therefore thin seedlings to two or three per module, for planting as a clump. They can be sown in September for harvesting through the winter under cover, even if this cover is only a simple layer of fleece.

Start harvesting after about two months, when the leaves of clumps are touching, or when you first notice flower stems. Clumps can be cut across the top or, much better, around their sides, for fortnightly harvests.

The main flowering happens in early spring: all the stems and flowering leaves can be eaten and look pretty in a bowl of mixed salad leaves.

TIP: Unpicked flowers quickly form hundreds of seeds, which can be collected by pulling a whole plant, hanging it to dry and then rubbing out the tiny seeds. Some seeds are always dropped in the garden and this salad plant often becomes a weed.

SEPTEMBER
week 3

SEPTEMBER
week 4

SEPTEMBER
Jobs for the month

When you are busy picking and preserving in September, remember it is the key month for sowing a wide range of salads for leaves through winter. Sow before mid-month so that plants can establish before it turns cold.

CLEARING: As soon as possible after any final harvests, remove all stems and leaves of vegetables that finish to make way for a final sowing of lamb's lettuce and plantings of salads such as oriental leaves.

WEEDING: As for July.

COMPOSTING: Compost may be spread where vegetables have finished and the ground is not needed for second sowings; and/or oriental leaves can be sown as an edible green manure.

SOWING INDOORS OR OUTDOORS: In the first week, a final sowing of lamb's lettuce, mizuna, rocket, mustards, leaf radish; also for lettuce and endive to overwinter indoors, followed – mid-month – by indoor sowings of all other winter salads for indoor leaves.

PLANTING: Salads for late autumn and for later covering with a cloche, spinach and then cabbage, onions, lettuce to overwinter in September's second half.

WATERING: Many summer vegetables such as beans, tomatoes and courgettes will now be winding down and need little more water. This is a good month (if dry) to water celeriac, leeks and other autumn or winter vegetables which will be bulking up in any warm autumn weather.

HARVESTING: Often the most abundant month, with an overlap of summer and autumn harvests, meaning a plethora of choices over what to eat.

September. From left: oriental leaves, leeks, chicories, beans, parsnips, cabbages.

OCTOBER

Any dry days in OCTOBER allow
you to harvest most summer and
winter vegetables, then clear beds
and rows after final pickings, and
spread compost on top of the clean
soil. Aim to have your beds looking
like chocolate cake, and keep them
weeded through winter. Before
the middle of the month, sow all
salads you want for winter, to grow
undercover if possible, for picking
until April. Wait another month
before planting broad beans.

Companion planting

This term is used for plants that grow better in close proximity. I have experimented with many of the classic combinations and still use a few such as planting French marigolds beside indoor tomatoes. The marigolds discourage aphids, their pattern of growing – low and bushy compared to the tall tomatoes – is complementary, and they look nice together.

By contrast, I have twice grown carrots between rows of onions and salad onions, because the smell of onions is supposed to deter carrot root flies. Yet those carrots had as many maggots in them as any others in the garden at that time – whereas the onions were superb! Thus certain suggestions for plant companions, while perhaps valid in certain combinations of soil and climate, may be invalid in others.

Probably the best method of companion planting is of a general rather than precise kind. Simply growing plants of many different families, interspersed with some flowers, thus creating a range of habitats for wildlife, is an excellent path to plant health and recreates every year a beautiful, enjoyable garden.

Vegetables as neighbours

It usually works better to keep small and large plants separate, especially in temperate climates, where light is important. This prevents shading of smaller leaves by larger ones, which may also offer a home to slugs, which will then have an easy passage to tender small plants.

Another good tip is to grow perennials such as rhubarb, globe artichokes and asparagus in one part of the garden or in one bed, and to group large annual vegetables together, separately from smaller salad plants, carrots, dwarf beans and bulb fennel. Second sowings and plantings of the small vegetables can then happen in clearer space with full light and moisture.

Some vegetables such as sweetcorn and climbing peas and beans pull moisture, and take light, from an area on either side of their row, so they need some clear soil around them with no leafy vegetables growing too close.

The polytunnel in September. Small French marigolds complement the growth of tall, cordon tomatoes and are one factor in reducing aphids.

Growing winter salads

Flavours of many salad plants become stronger in autumn. On the one hand is the heat and spiciness of oriental leaves and rocket, and on the other is bitterness from leaves of endive and chicory, a great health tonic for the liver. Bitterness can be offset by the pungency of mustards and can be mitigated by allowing endive and chicory hearts to develop, also by blanching (see page 128) and using a sweetened salad dressing.

Winter salads can have the greatest range of flavour, because more plants are in season then than in summer, including herbs such as chervil and coriander and strong-tasting leaves such as land cress.

For gentle heat in the salad bowl through autumn and winter, mizuna, pak choi and Chinese cabbage all have a nice balance of juiciness, crunch and mild pungency. Milder heat comes from leaves of young plants; then, after 2–3 months' growth, leaves of some plants become extra spicy and hot, especially wild rocket and 'Green in the Snow' mustard. For a milder mustard try 'Red Frills', which also looks wonderful, both in the garden and on the plate.

Spinach has a flavour all its own, more agreeable than chard, and spinach leaves are noticeably sweet in late winter after frosts have helped some sugars to develop. Try chewing winter salad leaves thoroughly to let their flavours fill your mouth with a sweet aftertaste, especially after it has been frosty. Extra sweetness is a wonderful foil for the pungent mustards and bitter endives. You find milder flavours in winter purslane and lamb's lettuce.

Mizuna 'Red Knight' and mustards 'Green in the Snow' and 'Red Frills'.

Decorative salads

Many winter salad leaves have great decorative value as well as wonderful flavour. The ferny leaves of chervil have a beautiful delicacy about them even though they are surprisingly hardy, and beet and chard leaves have an attractive sculptural quality.

There are also striking red varieties of kale, komatsuna, beet, chard, mizuna, mustards and other oriental leaves that add welcome colour to a winter salad.

OCTOBER
weeks 1 & 2

Making your own compost

Home-made compost is often more full of life-enhancing bacteria and fungi than many over-heated commercial composts. There are many ways to create compost, but these are answers to some of the questions I am most frequently asked about composting.

What are the best ingredients?

Good results come from a mix of green and brown ingredients. Green ingredients are sappy, fresh leaves, trimmings and plants; brown ingredients are dead or dry organic matter and any soil on plant roots. Few gardens have the perfect combination – about six parts green to four parts brown – available at all times, so compost quality and the time needed to make it are always variable.

What ingredients can be used?

Any plant matter – fresh, dry or processed. So you can add: weeds, including roots of perennials; vegetable and fruit peelings including citrus; paper (preferably crumpled) and non-shiny cardboard; animal manure; wood ash; vacuum cleaner bags except when they contain plastic; and soil in only small amounts. I advise breaking or cutting any larger ingredients into lengths of no more than 10–15cm (4–6in).

What can't be composted?

Plastic, metal, glass, thick pieces of wood, large stems, evergreen leaves and seeding weed heads.

Is it better to have an open heap or an enclosed bin?

Compost can be made successfully in either open or closed heaps, though most small gardens, with occasional ingredients, will benefit from a closed bin to keep the garden tidy. Covers and lids are good for retaining heat and moisture, and for excluding excess rainfall, especially on finished heaps when they are maturing. A plastic sheet is cheap and easy to remove and reuse, while cardboard also makes a good cover. Avoid modern carpets as they contain too many chemicals.

Do ingredients need to be layered or mixed?

In a word 'no', although making layers of different ingredients is often advised. This applies only when you are adding a lot of one green material such as grass mowings or weeds, which compost much better when alternated with something brown such as crumpled paper, to prevent the green ingredients from packing into an airless lump. It also provides the brown ingredients with enough nitrogen to break down. Good results come from adapting the basic principle of half green, half brown to whatever materials you have.

continued ▶▶

Why is air so important?

Oxygen is an absolutely vital ingredient. Too much green at one time, squashing out the air, causes sogginess and smelly putrefaction instead of warm, sweet decomposition. Bacteria do a lot of the work initially and they need oxygen to multiply, which is why compost can be made extremely fast when the heap is regularly turned to admit fresh air.

Do heaps have to be turned?

If you have time to wait for compost to mature – about one year – then turning is not necessary. Heaps that are turned once, about a month after the final ingredients were added, develop into more even and sweeter-smelling compost, partly because of the mixing and partly because of bacteria being fed by the newly introduced air.

Is an activator needed?

I have tried several proprietary activators without noticing a significant difference to the composting process. Adding some animal manure or urine is the cheapest and most effective way of ensuring healthy composting; poultry manure is a most invaluable ingredient, better composted than spread in a fresh state over the soil.

Is watering necessary?

Extra moisture is required only in hot summers when half or more of the ingredients are dry rather than soft and sappy. More problems are caused by a heap being too wet than too dry, so when watering dry ingredients use a fine rose to disperse small amounts evenly. Except in freak hot summers, I advise against watering heaps.

How long before compost is ready?

Be patient. One year from start to finish is sufficient time for most of a heap to be usable; or, if a heap is turned, compost can be ready in six months. Heaps made in spring and summer mature more quickly than those assembled in autumn and winter, partly because of higher ambient temperature and also because many warm-weather ingredients are green rather than brown, which decompose more quickly.

When can a heap be used?

Good compost is dark brown, soft, moist but not soggy, more or less crumbly and pleasant smelling. When most of a heap is at this stage of decomposition, probably with some red brandlings (worms) at the bottom, I would use it, while forking any less decomposed ingredients into a new heap.

What if compost is sodden and smelly?

Too much moisture and too little air leads to putrefaction. This means that you have added a lot more green than brown; or too much rain has entered the heap; or there is poor drainage in the soil at its base. A remedy is to turn the whole heap to reintroduce air, cover it and leave it for two months in summer or half a year in winter, before spreading it on the soil.

What if it is dry and fibrous?

Introducing moisture evenly is not easy because water simply tends to run through a dry heap. I suggest watering lightly every day for a week, with a fine rose; or turning the heap and watering gently in stages as you move it.

Compost at different stages of decomposition: the current heap is at the back, the oldest compost at the front under cardboard.

SPECIAL CASES

- Large amounts of pernicious roots such as bindweed can be composted, but preferably in a light-proof bin and with enough other material to speed up their decay before they can grow again.
- Weeds with viable seeds are better burnt, because few domestic compost heaps attain enough heat (around 65°C/150°F – hot enough to burn the skin) to kill them. This problem will lessen as your garden becomes cleaner of weeds, and fewer weeds are close to seeding when cleared.
- Seeds of some garden flowers or herbs such as forget-me-not, foxglove, pot marigold and feverfew often survive composting. Although these plants are less noxious than many weeds, their sheer number means some extra hoeing will be needed when they emerge as tiny seedlings.
- Most diseased leaves can be safely added, including those infected with blight and mildew; and vegetables with pest damage (and the pests!) are safe to compost. But alliums infected with white rot around their roots, and onions with neck rot are best burnt.
- Large amounts of leaves are better piled in a separate heap, where they will turn brown and fibrous after at least a year. Nutrient levels in pure leafmould are not high unless some animal manure can be mixed with it, to add nitrogen to its carbon.

Mulching
to control weeds

Although mulches can be laid at any time, autumn is the best season to carry out this task, in preparation for the next season's cropping. Weed-suppressing mulches will be most effective if they are applied at any time in autumn and winter, before new growth begins.

Mulches for suppressing perennial weeds

First of all, cover the area with compost and manure to give a soft, fertile surface for subsequent sowing and planting. The soil is enriched as well as cleared: worms, bacteria and fungi love to be busy under dark mulches. Then top this with a covering that will exclude light totally. The most popular options are discussed below.

CARDBOARD: This freely available waste product slowly decomposes *in situ* and adds to soil life. Large pieces of thick cardboard are the most useful and their edges should overlap by 15cm (6in). Take care to remove tape and staples first and avoid cardboard that is laminated with thin layers of plastic.

BLACK PLASTIC: This is an effective light-excluding mulch and can be reused many times. Unless it is of the more expensive, woven kind, black plastic does not allow water through, so is best put on when ground is damp. Plastic sheets should stay on for one growing season if the soil is choked with perennial weeds, to weaken all the roots.

STRAW OR GRASS TRIMMINGS: You can mulch with layers of straw and lawn mowings, but in time these become permeable to light and allow the more persistent weeds to regrow. They may also introduce some new weed seeds.

NEWSPAPER: This is difficult to use because of its smaller pieces, which take time to lay, and blow around more easily than other mulches, but it can be kept in place with 2.5cm (1in) of compost.

CARPETS: Pure wool carpet is excellent for mulching weeds, but nearly all carpets are now full of synthetic fibre that disintegrates into horrible fragments, as sunlight gradually degrades it. Non-wool carpets can also contain chemicals that are best avoided.

Keeping a mulch in place

Sheet mulches can be weighted with stones or stakes, and in the case of cardboard with lumps of compost and manure at the corners and along edges. Cardboard rots more quickly under weights so don't overdo it. It can be covered completely with compost but does degrade quickly.

After mulching

Mulches that decompose, such as cardboard and straw, usually need another layer applied after 2–3 months, depending on the weather, how thick the initial layer was and what weeds it was covering. Weeds such as couch grass will need up to three applications of organic mulch, or a 6- to 9-month covering with black polythene.

After the period of time suggested peek under your mulch to check that there are no green leaves. A few perennial weeds may be weakly present, with some of their pale white roots visible near the surface, drawn upwards in search of light. You can ease these roots out with a trowel, pulling at the same time as levering the trowel, to remove most from the top 10cm (4in) of soil.

Slugs like the moisture under mulches and may be numerous for a month or two after polythene is removed, depending on the weather. Take extra precautions during that time and avoid planting slug-prone vegetables straightaway after clearing an area.

You can plant direct into mulched soil, preferably with compost on top. However, always persist with removing any regrowth of perennial weeds, because if you leave just a few stems of couch grass or bindweed to enlarge and lengthen they will soon recolonise a large area – I have seen it happen too often. Provided you persevere with weeding, you are in sight of having really clean soil for easy vegetable growing. Make the most of it!

MULCHING TO CONTROL WEEDS AND PROVIDE IMMEDIATE PLANTING POSSIBILITIES

1 In January, a challenging crop of weeds included couch, dandelion, buttercup and bindweed under a newly erected polytunnel.

2 To suppress and control the weeds I used a combination of cardboard on the grass, then 7cm (3in) of year-old manure and topsoil.

3 In April I put another 5cm (2in) of different composts on top of the original 7cm (3in) layer, over the paths and the beds.

4 By mid-June, mulch had suppressed the grass and all weeds except bindweed, while vegetable growth had become abundant.

OCTOBER
weeks 3 & 4

OCTOBER
Jobs for the month

It helps to see October as a busy first month of the vegetable growing year, with some plantings for early harvests next summer, and using every spare moment to clear ground, spread compost and be prepared for spring.

CLEARING: Many vegetables finish in October, including courgette and squash plants, summer beans, lettuce, sweetcorn, tomato, cucumber, aubergine and pepper. Remove all weeds as you go, and cut all cleared vegetable stems to 15cm (6in) length before composting them.

WEEDING: Weeds including bindweed will be losing vigour, but grasses and chickweed can still flower and set seed, so pull any you see, by hand, because soil is usually too damp for hoeing during the month of October.

COMPOSTING: You can spread compost and manure as soon as ground has been cleared; or if planting garlic and broad beans you can dib them in first and then spread compost or manure on top of the cloves and bean seeds.

SOWING/PLANTING: Garlic cloves are best planted in early October and broad bean seeds at month's end or in early November, the vegetable year's final sowing; also plant salads under cover by mid-October if possible, so that plants have time to root properly before winter.

WATERING: Needed for dry soil under cover after pulling out summer vegetables such as tomatoes. Be sure to water thoroughly, often for longer than you would imagine, to be sure of the soil being moist before you plant winter vegetables.

HARVESTING: Another month of abundance even though many summer vegetables have finished, being replaced by parsnip, celeriac, cabbage, leek, Brussels sprouts and squash.

October harvests boast an overlap of summer and winter vegetables.

NOVEMBER

Access to the plot may be limited
in NOVEMBER by poor weather,
but there should be a lot to pick,
from cabbage and kale to parsnips,
celeriac, beetroot and salads until
frost arrives in earnest. After that
you can still be cutting lamb's
lettuce, and salads under cover.
Roots, except for parsnips, are best
harvested and stored by the middle
of the month, as they will remain
in better condition well away
from wet soil.

Crop rotation

I do not rotate crops in the traditional way, finding it better to grow what I need and then leaving as long a gap as possible – which may be only two years – between vegetable families such as legumes, brassicas, potatoes, alliums and umbellifers. (Note that 'roots' are not a family, so counting them as a group makes no sense in terms of a rotation to avoid disease.)

When growing vegetables you need to bear rotation in mind, without letting it dictate what you grow. There are several groups with family associations. Within each group, plants are susceptible to similar pests and diseases, which can be reduced by growing vegetables of the same family in different places each year as far as is practical. In the table below you can see which of the main vegetable crops belong to the same family.

I know many gardeners who successfully ignore rotation altogether: for example, by growing tomatoes in the same greenhouse soil each year. When rotating minimally, adding compost and manure does help to keep soil, and so plants, in good health.

FAMILY: common name/Latin name*	VEGETABLES** and common herbs
Alliums/Alliaceae	Chive, garlic, leek, onion, salad onion, shallot
Asparagaceae	Asparagus
Beets/Chenopodiaceae	Beetroot, chard, leaf beet, orach, spinach
Brassicas/Brassicaceae	Broccoli, Brussels sprout, cabbage, cauliflower, kohl rabi, land cress, oriental leaves, radish, rocket, swede, turnip
Cucurbits/Cucurbitaceae	Courgette, cucumber, melon, squash
Grass/Poaceae	Sweetcorn
Legumes/Fabaciae	Broad bean, French bean, runner bean, peas
Lettuces/Daisy/Asteraceae	Artichokes (globe and Jerusalem), chicory, endive, lettuce
Mint/Lamiaceae	Basil, Chinese artichoke, marjoram, mint, rosemary, sage, thyme
Polygonaceae	Rhubarb, sorrel
Solanums/Solanaceae	Aubergine, chilli, pepper, potato, tomato
Umbellifers/Umbelliferaceae	Carrot, celery, celeriac, chervil, coriander, dill, fennel, parsley, parsnip
Valerianaceae	Lamb's lettuce (corn salad)

* I have included more than one name where several are commonly used.
** Vegetables not mentioned are winter purslane, related to claytonia wildflowers of North America, and summer purslane, which is related to wild moss roses.

Growing
perennial vegetables

These vegetables need sowing and/or planting only once, for harvests over many years. However, they still need a fair amount of maintenance such as weeding and tidying. It is important to plant into soil that has been cleaned of all perennial weeds, especially couch grass, because of the difficulty of removing such weeds once the vegetables are established.

October is a good time of year to increase your stock of globe artichokes and rhubarb by root division. Use a sharp spade to slice some root(s) and a small part of the main stem off the edge of healthy, well-established plants, and plant them straightaway in clean soil where they are to grow.

Globe artichoke

WHERE & WHEN TO SOW: Sow indoors March–April.

TIME FROM SOWING TO PLANTING: 4–6 weeks.

WHEN TO PLANT & SPACING: May; 75–90cm (30–36in).

TIP: You can also plant roots in autumn or spring. This easy vegetable needs considerable space.

Asparagus

WHERE & WHEN TO SOW: Sow indoors March–April.

TIME FROM SOWING TO PLANTING: 8–10 weeks with potting on.

WHEN TO PLANT & SPACING: Summer; 90cm (36in).

TIP: You can plant purchased crowns March–early April.

It is not difficult to grow asparagus plants from seed, but it adds a year to the 2–3 years you need to wait for a first harvest, compared to when you plant roots, which are called crowns. While these plants are growing, be sure to clean their planting patch of all weeds. Rather than using the ridges sometimes recommended, I plant on flat ground: harvests are good and weeding is easier.

Rhubarb

WHERE & WHEN TO SOW: Sow indoors March–April.

TIME FROM SOWING TO PLANTING: 8–10 weeks with potting on.

WHEN TO PLANT & SPACING: Summer; 90cm (36in).

TIP: You can plant a piece of root in autumn, and through the winter before February.

If a neighbour or friend has good rhubarb, they may be persuaded to let you slice a large root or two off their clump when the rhubarb is dormant.

Otherwise sow seeds in spring, as for asparagus, although they grow more quickly. After potting on and planting out by July, you may have good-sized plants by the following spring, allowing a light picking in their first season.

Make your own wooden beds

Now that winter is virtually upon us and there is rather less to do in the garden, it is a good time to get ready for the next growing season by making some wooden beds. These are two of my ideas for beds 15cm (6in) deep.

Wooden bed with posts

One way to create wooden beds is by hammering four 30cm (12in) lengths of 5 x 5cm (2 x 2in) square posts at each corner of your proposed bed, 10–12cm (4–5in) into the soil, as in project one (right). Keep checking that the bed corners are square by measuring each diagonal to the same length. If they are different, adjust the corners and also recheck that the sides' and ends' length correspond to those of your prepared timber planks.

Assemble bed sides by screwing or nailing four planks to the outside of four corner pegs. Extra pegs for the midpoint of the sides' outer edges will be needed if planks are longer than 1.2m (4ft) or thinner than 5cm (2in), to prevent the wood from bowing out under pressure of the weight of compost inside.

Wooden bed with braces

A simpler idea is a bed that is held together with braces, as in project two (right). For each bed of 2.4 x 1.2m (8 x 4ft), buy three lengths of 2.4m (8ft) wood, 15cm (6in) wide and 2.5cm (1in) thick. Two of the planks are for the sides, and the third one is sawn in half to provide the ends. They can be screwed together at the four corners using 90-degree braces, either inside the frame or on the outside.

Then simply lay this frame in position and fill it with suitable compost. There is no need to prepare the ground in any way, because the depth of organic matter will be enough to kill most green growth. But thinner coverings of organic matter, say 5–7cm (2–3in), will need a light-excluding mulch on top, such as cardboard (see page 162).

Just one month after this bed was created, on undisturbed grass, and planted up, the module-raised salad plants are flourishing.

PROJECT ONE: WOODEN BED WITH POSTS

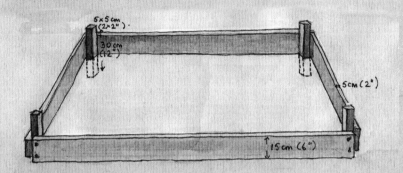

5x5cm
(2x2").

30cm
(12")

5cm (2")

15cm (6")

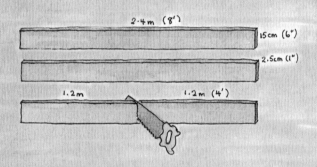

2·4m (8')

15cm (6")

2.5cm (1")

1·2m

1·2m (4')

PROJECT TWO: WOODEN BED WITH BRACES

Types of compost & manure

The words 'compost' and 'manure' can mislead because they describe such a wide range of materials. Manure is mostly now understood as coming from animals, yet the word is occasionally used for synthetic fertilizers. The descriptions below are to clarify what you can use.

Compost

Compost is the dark-coloured residue of decomposed plant materials and animal excretions. Variable ingredients, assembled in different ways and at different times of year, make composts of vastly different qualities.

GARDEN COMPOST: A variable product! Any gardener with a little space for a heap or container, and some raw materials, should have a go at making some. For help with this, see page 159.

GREEN WASTE COMPOST: This is from the hot fermentation of household and garden wastes. Powerful shredders chop all ingredients, including woody ones, into small enough pieces for rapid heating to occur, so that few weed seeds and pathogens survive. It is easy to use but the large percentage of woody ingredients means fewer nutrients, unless some food waste has been added; or spread some animal manure with it.

MUSHROOM COMPOST: A 'waste product' after it has been used to grow crops of mushrooms in dark sheds or tunnels. The ingredients are mainly straw, with some horse or chicken manure, peat, chalk and plenty of fungal mycelium. There are fewer nutrients than in animal manures.

MULTIPURPOSE POTTING COMPOST: A concentrated growing medium for plants in trays, pots, containers and growing bags sold by the sack and of uncertain quality. It is now often green waste compost, mixed with nutrient-rich ingredients; previously, it was made with peat. Multipurpose compost is expensive for spreading in the garden; if you do, be sure to use organic compost, as its nutrients will not leach away in winter or in heavy rain.

VERMICOMPOST: This consists of worm casts, and is the dark, soft residue of worm farming (or of worm-eaten garden compost or animal manure). It forms a rich and soft compost.

Manure

Manure is excrement from animals such as horses, cows, pigs, sheep and poultry, together with any bedding they have lain on – usually one or more of cereal straw, shredded paper, hemp and wood shavings.

The value of manure depends on how long it has been composted, how much bedding was used and of which kind, and whether the heap has been looked after (for example, with no weeds being allowed to seed in it). There are great possibilities in any animal manure that has spent several months in a tidy heap.

Fresh manure, with its identifiable ingredients of animal faeces and undecomposed bedding, should be composted in a heap for 4–6 months at least, or up to a year for best results, until it is generally dark brown and showing signs of becoming crumbly.

Chemical residues can cause problems: for example if the animals' food has included grass or hay from pastures sprayed with herbicides containing aminopyralids. A farmer should be able to tell you if asked, but horse owners probably won't know how the hay was grown.

A TRIAL OF COMPOSTS

One July I potted four one-month-old lettuce plants into four pots of different composts and manure. The composts were: green waste and multipurpose compost in the front (left to right), and manure and my own compost at the back (left to right). The plants grew until November and I harvested some outer leaves every three weeks from all except the lettuce in green waste compost. No liquid feed was used.

My own garden compost nourished the strongest, longest-growing plant compared with those growing in manure or multipurpose compost: lettuce in the latter grew fast in the first month and then weakened. The green waste compost supported a weak yellow plant at first, but its colour (not size) improved after two months when some of the wood in the compost had finished decomposing.

11 August: four plants of lettuce 'Mottistone', in pots of four different composts at the start of the test.

19 August: the same lettuce, having put on unequal amounts of growth.

Mid-September before the second pick: no feeds were given at any stage.

Mid-October: the green waste compost is finally releasing some nutrients.

How to grow:
BROAD BEANS

Autumn sowing

WHERE & WHEN TO SOW: Sow direct late October to December; or under cover in pots or modules in mid- to late November for planting out in February.

SPACING: 5 x 38cm (2 x 15in); dib holes 5cm (2in) deep or draw a drill of that depth.

CARE: The first harvests of broad beans in June are an exciting, early taste of summer. Earliest harvests are from autumn sowing, but overwintered plants, which prefer free-draining soils, are at some risk of succumbing to bad weather: dry winters are better than wet ones. Spring frosts are not a problem but severe winter frost may kill plants. 'Aquadulce Claudia' is the best variety for overwintering and has large, pale beans.

Outdoor sowings in late October for cold areas to December in mild areas can be covered with mesh, net or brushwood placed on top, to stop birds pulling out plants just shooting. Spring sowings and plantings, from February to May outdoors, can be covered with fleece for 4–6 weeks to trap warmth.

Beans have different flavours at all stages. Young pods can be eaten whole, and you can rub the skins off mature, starchy beans after immersing them for a few minutes in boiling water, to leave a dense, creamy kernel. Some 2–3 weeks are needed for tender, fully edible pods to mature into dark green and brown pods with starchy beans.

Spring sowing

WHERE & WHEN TO SOW: Sow direct February–May, or indoors January–May.

TIME FROM SOWING TO PLANTING: 3–6 weeks.

WHEN TO PLANT & SPACING: March–May; 10 x 38cm (4 x 15in).

Spring flowers: broad beans.

TIP: Pinch off the tops of plants when they are in full flower; these tips are very good to eat when lightly cooked. Pinching out the tops also helps to avoid infestations of black aphids by depriving them of a landing place, because they don't like landing on bare-topped stems.

NOVEMBER
weeks 1 & 2

NOVEMBER
weeks 3 & 4

NOVEMBER
Jobs for the month

November is really a continuation of October with the important theme of cleaning and preparing both ground and yourself for winter. Although the weather is often gloomy, being outside is good for soul and body.

CLEARING: Larger stems and leaves, including asparagus, are best cleared to a compost heap, while smaller debris such as parsnip, leek and endive leaves can be left *in situ* and covered with compost as soon as harvests have been taken.

WEEDING: If you have kept on top of weeds throughout the spring, summer and autumn there should be very few weeds to deal with, but keep tweaking out any small grasses, cleavers, dandelions, etc.

COMPOSTING: Continue as before so that more and more of the plot is covered as harvests finish. You can also spread compost around growing plants such as kale.

HARVESTING: Fresh harvests include spinach, chard, the last calabrese, parsnip, swede, leeks, salad leaves (including pak choi, tatsoi, mustards, rocket, chervil, endive, chicory, spinach), carrot, beetroot, celeriac, turnip – and the last four can now be harvested to store, especially if hard frost is forecast.

November salads of leaf radish, 'Red Dragon' mustard and red mizuna, all sown in August.

DECEMBER

Cold, dry days in DECEMBER are
good for spreading your remaining
compost and manure before
Christmas, so that frost can break
up any lumps and help make a
soft surface for next year. Back
indoors, reflect on the receding year
and plan improvements for the
next one; above all, aim to build
more health into your soil so that
plants can better resist whatever
comes their way.

Chicory
for forcing

Chicory is a particularly useful salad plant to grow as it has such a wide variety of uses. Plants sown in early to midsummer can be grown in the open garden either for loose leaves or to form hearts. A favourite winter salad is forced chicory, which forms plump, creamy white chicons.

Look for Witloof varieties such as 'Witloof de Brussels' or the newer F1 hybrid 'Zoom' when forcing chicory, and sow outside or indoors from mid-May to early June. These plants need a whole season of growth, but there is a risk of them flowering if they are sown too early. One option is a late-May sowing in modules or pots indoors, sowing two seeds per pot and later thinning the seedlings to the strongest plant. This allows you to make an earlier sowing of spinach or radish and plant out the chicory in the same place after you have harvested the spinach or radish in late June.

Blanching chicons

The chicory plants will grow large by autumn, with bulky roots that can be harvested and brought indoors for forcing. Dig up the roots in late autumn or early winter (definitely before Christmas) and cut off all leaves to put on the compost heap. Pot on the roots in a bucket filled with partly or fully rotted organic matter, and place the bucket (or buckets) in a dark cupboard at room temperature. This will produce harvests of tight, creamy yellow chicons within 3–5 weeks, and there will be smaller second harvests after that, until April at the latest. By depriving the growth of light, the chicons will not only be pale in colour but also more tender and with much less bitterness than plants grown in full light.

It is a good idea to keep a stock of roots in lightly moist sand in a cool shed and force just a few at a time as you need them, to ensure a winter-long supply.

Forced chicory

DECEMBER
weeks 1, 2, 3 & 4

Pests in winter

While common pests of the spring and summer such as aphids and caterpillars are not such a problem in the winter months, unfortunately not all pests lie low in the dormant season.

Birds

Wood pigeons are usually the main bird problem at this time of year; damage is most dramatic in cold winters, so be ready to cover plants if severe frost and snow are likely. I find that the best protection is afforded by mesh on top of plants, or a net suspended above susceptible plants, chiefly brassicas.

Plastic netting with 2.5–5cm (1–2in) mesh – larger holes are better to let snow through – can be draped over stakes with upside-down plastic pots on top, or over large cloche hoops spaced at 1.2m (4ft) intervals. The netting needs to be held about 45cm (18in) above the plants so that pigeons cannot land on top and peck through the net.

Netting to prevent pigeons is best suspended above plants.

Rabbits

Damage from rabbits can occur at any time of year, but most noticeably in winter and early spring. Salads of all kinds, brassicas, some umbellifers and alliums are all at risk.

Beds of susceptible plants can be covered with mesh, or the whole plot can be fenced, but this is tedious to install because you need either to bury it to about 30cm (12in), or to run it over the soil surface outwards from the fence-line, for about 60cm (24in), to prevent rabbits digging underneath.

Mice

Nibbling of roots and flower bulbs or disappearing vegetable seeds suggest mice are the culprits. They tend to move into sheds, greenhouses and roof spaces in search of shelter and easy pickings as the weather grows colder. They can be controlled by setting traps.

Deer & badgers

Browsing deer can destroy many plants, but the remedy is expensive and time-consuming – a 2.5m (8ft) metal mesh fence. Some netting as for birds may keep them out of particular crops.

Badgers also need a solid fence or wall to deter them, because they are hugely strong and surprisingly agile. Most of the time badgers are more messy than destructive.

Working with the moon

Gardening by the moon is something that almost everybody practises differently, and I hesitate to offer precise advice. It is a fascinating topic and a great way to become familiar with less visible influences on growth.

There are so many possibilities, according to whether the moon is waxing or waning, ascending or descending, and in which constellation it resides. But which of these has more importance?

I have done a few moon experiments, of variable outcome. They mostly demonstrate an influence, but less predictably than I understand. Below are the results of one in which I sowed carrots on two different days, deemed suitable and unsuitable in *The Biodynamic Sowing and Planting Calendar*, by Maria and Matthias Thun, published annually by Floris Books. Their advice concentrates mainly on constellations in which the moon resides at the time of sowing, rather than moon phases such as waxing and waning.

Other research has pointed to more vigorous growth of plants sown when the moon is waxing, especially in the few days before a full moon. In the experiment below, 12 April was a waning moon and 19 April was waxing, so perhaps this had an effect.

CARROTS 'EARLY NANTES'

In September 2009 I made a bed of 1.2 x 2.4m (4 x 8ft), by filling a wooden frame with well-rotted cow manure on top of grass and surfacing it with a 3cm (1¼in) layer of fine compost. I grew salads in it that autumn.

In April I measured the bed and divided it into two equal halves, A and B, and sowed carrots 'Early Nantes', to compare moon days given in *The Biodynamic Sowing and Planting Calender*:

A was sown on a 'bad' day, 12 April (in the book shown by dashed lines, sow nothing).
B was sown on a 'root' day with the moon in Taurus, 19 April.

It was a dry spring, I watered occasionally, and there was no carrot root fly. Harvests were as in the table, left, with a first weighing on 29 July of one row from each half. (To convert, 1kg equals 2.2lb.)

	A	B	
29 July	1.6	1.8	
12 August	1.8	2.4	
26 August	1.9	2.3	more forked roots in A
2 September	2.4	2.6	last rows, similar quality
Total	7.7kg	9.1kg	

SUMMARY: 20 per cent more roots on B, an earth day sowing, although it was a week later. The quality of roots was mostly similar.

Buying composts & manures

Few gardens are large enough to produce all the compost they will need simply from the waste products of the garden and kitchen, so it is very likely you will need to buy in organic matter at some stage. Take care when buying, as labels may be misleading: for example, I bought a sack of 'Organic Farmyard Manure' which, when opened, revealed itself as woody, green waste compost. Bags coming from a 'farm' with photos of animals may not contain animal manure!

Commercial composts

GREEN WASTE COMPOSTS: These are of extremely variable quality, even when they look quite similar; in Britain, they must at least meet the PAS 100 guidelines, a certified industry standard. Usually the heaps have been hot enough to kill all weed residues and any pathogens, but the heat may also have been intense enough to 'cook' the compost, almost carbonizing it, leaving it with a possible lack of bacteria and fungi.

MUSHROOM COMPOST: Pesticide residues may linger in mushroom compost, although more mushroom farmers now use predators to control their pests, and some grow organically. The compost has great value as a weed-free mulch, and it enriches soil with lively organic matter. If it is light brown and strawy when purchased or delivered, I suggest you leave it in a heap to decompose further for 2–3 months, unless it is to be used for mulching bushes and borders.

ANIMAL MANURES: These have more nutrients, but their quality and ease of use are variable, according to their age and the kind of animal and type of bedding used: straw, for example, helps the manure to rot more quickly than a bedding of wood shavings.

WORM COMPOST: This is excellent for growing plants in pots or containers, or for improving all soils. Use it sparingly, because it is expensive to produce: a lot of worms are needed to make a small amount of compost, and home wormeries require careful and time-consuming management!

Value for money

Quality and ease of use vary so much that value for money is hard to assign. Year-old animal manure is more valuable than green waste compost, in which the main ingredients are less rich in nutrients. One tonne is enough for spreading 2–3cm ($^3/_4$–$1^1/_4$in) of compost or manure on a 60–80m (200–260ft) length of beds which are 1.2m (4ft) wide, or half to two-thirds of a 10-rod allotment. There can be 12- to 30-wheelbarrow loads per tonne, depending on the size of your barrow.

For a first season of thick mulching (7–10cm/3–4in), to improve soil and reduce weed growth, a 6-tonne load would be needed to cover the beds of a 10-rod allotment. Thereafter, 1–2 tonnes per annum is enough to keep improving the soil, which can be supplied with two or three home-made heaps if they are being filled from a larger garden, for instance with grass and leaves.

You cannot make enough compost just from the residues of a vegetable plot.

A major part of the cost of organic matter is transport, so if you can collect it in your own trailer, unbagged, it will be much cheaper; many car trailers hold more than half a tonne. If someone offers to deliver a 'trailerload', check how heavy it will be to have an idea of quantity.

Green waste compost with bits of wood.

Ease of use

Mushroom and green waste compost are mostly soft, fluffy and easy to spread, with few large lumps. Home-made compost and animal manures are often lumpier, but if spread in autumn and lightly raked during winter, to break up the lumps, they can become fine and of good consistency for spring sowing and planting.

Lumpy compost can be spread as a mulch around vegetables that are already growing, such as courgettes, climbing beans and brassicas, and between rows of parsnips, celeriac, carrots, leeks and garlic. It will finish decomposing as they grow and improve the soil for a succeeding vegetable.

One-year-old mushroom compost for potting.

When you see lots of brandling worms, the manure or compost is ideal for spreading on the soil.

Horse manure with many weed seedlings.

Storing vegetables for winter

Storing vegetables is a continual process which starts in summer after harvesting garlic, in early July, and onions, in August, both of which can be kept until April or May if fully dry. Later there are more crops to deal with.

Potatoes

Prepare for storage by leaving potato tubers on top of the soil for a day (if fine) to dry their skins before placing in sacks where they should keep all winter out of any frost.

Squash

Winter squash should mature on the plant, until their skins and stems are hard and dry. Cut and handle each squash carefully, storing them indoors in the warm and dry.

Roots

I keep celeriac and turnips in wooden boxes, beetroot and carrots in paper sacks as cool as possible (but without too much freezing – especially the carrots). Root vegetables can also be stored in the soil, unless you live in an area of regular hard frosts below -5°C (23°F).

Brassicas

Leaf vegetables are a winter treasure when greens are scarce, and they are mostly brassicas such as kale, Brussels sprouts and 'January King' or Savoy cabbages. All of these can be left outside to harvest fresh when needed, as long as they are protected from wildlife. Earlier white and red cabbages which heart firmly in autumn are best cut in November and stored in boxes as cool as possible, then trimmed before use. Leeks are frost-hardy and keep growing until April, especially winter varieties such as 'Bandit', 'Apollo' and 'Musselburgh'. However in frosty areas you can harvest a month's supply in milder spells, with their roots and some soil left on, to store in boxes.

Salads

Many salad plants survive winter, from sowings in August and September, but plants growing outside with no protection will grow only a few, small leaves from Christmas until March or even April, except for land cress and lamb's lettuce. Salads protected by a cloche, polytunnel or greenhouse, and even just fleeced in mild winters, will give steady harvests, especially after light increases in mid-February.

These onions and garlic were photographed on 31 March, 6–8 months after harvest.

DECEMBER
Jobs for the month

Bring a festive feeling of thankfulness to your December garden, when there is time to weigh up the year's results. As ground becomes bare, take a good look at the plot and imagine some better ways to grow vegetables.

CLEARING: Similar to November, meaning that most of the plot is clear and composted by Christmas, with the rest of the ground growing harvests for winter.

HARVESTING: Brussels sprouts, savoy cabbage, kale, leeks, parsnip, swede, chicory roots for forcing, salads such as lamb's lettuce, land cress and winter purslane; also stored endive and radicchio and some leaves from plants under cover.

MULCHING: The year and this book end where they began, with an emphasis on rich healthy soil. More than most other plants, vegetables repay you with abundant growth when given soil covered with well-rotted organic matter. There are so many improvements in yield, continuity of harvests, flavour, speed of growth, resistance to pests and weeds pulling out easily – and the enjoyment of gardening increases.

Kale growing in the orchard under a snow-covered net.

Suppliers & resources

FERRYMAN POLYTUNNELS LTD, Westleigh, Morchard Road, Nr Crediton, Devon EX17 5LS (www.ferrymanpolytunnels.co.uk) sells a wide range of polytunnels in widths of 2.4–7.3m (8–24ft), lengths in any multiple of 1.5m (5ft) and heights of 2.1–3m (7–10ft).

HIGH-QUALITY COPPER TOOLS can be found at www.implementations.co.uk, PO Box 2568, Nuneaton, CV10 9YR.

LBS HORTICULTURE LTD, Standroyd Mill, Cottontree, Colne, Lancs BB8 7BW (www.lbsbuyersguide.co.uk) carries a wide and good-value range of useful accessories, including netting, mesh, fleece, plug/module trays and polytunnels.

OSMO OIL AND PAINT, all of natural materials, give excellent protection to the wood of raised beds and greenhouses: Unit 24, Anglo Business Park, Smeaton Close, Aylesbury HP19 8UP (www.osmouk.com).

CHASE ORGANICS LTD, Riverdene, Molesey Road, Hersham, KT12 4RG (www.organiccatalogue.com) for seeds, gardening aids, comfrey roots, etc.

ORGANIC COMPOST for plant raising from West Riding Organics Ltd, Halifax Road, Littleborough, Lancs OL15 0LF (www.wrorganics.co.uk).

FOR STARTING OUT, including materials and emailed reminders, have a look at www.quickcrop.co.uk.

PLUG AND MODULE TRAYS are much harder to buy than should be the case. B&Q sell sturdy, 60-cell plug trays in packs of three (www.diy.com).

ORGANIC PLANTS from Delfland Nurseries, Benwick Road, Doddington, March PE15 0TU (www.organicplants.co.uk): an excellent range and with good advice.

BIODYNAMIC AGRICULTURAL ASSOCIATION, Painswick Inn, Gloucester Street, Stroud GL5 1QG (www.biodynamic.org.uk) for information and supply of preparations.

Books

Maria and Matthias Thun, *The Biodynamic Sowing and Planting Calendar*, Floris Books, published annually.

Charles Dowding, *Organic Gardening: The Natural No-Dig Way*, Green Books (second edition, 2010).

Charles Dowding, *Salad Leaves For All Seasons*, Green Books (2008).

Charles Dowding, *How to Grow Winter Vegetables*, Green Books (2011).

Charles Dowding's Vegetable Course, Frances Lincoln (2012)

www.charlesdowding.co.uk has much information on vegetable growing, no-dig and Charles's courses.